"I've been a client of Jeff's for a couple of years and wholly appreciate the authenticity and sincerity he brings to our relationship. As a customer, I recommend the philosophies in this book wholeheartedly."

—Jamel Jones,
Senior Director of Business Information
Systems at Comcast

"I've been on the cutting edge of sales and AI for years, so I can especially appreciate the value of being human in sales. Jeff captures the essence of what great salespeople need to keep in mind, and it is great advice for anyone who negotiates for themself in anything in life—which is pretty much all of us."

—Scott Britton,
Co-Founder, Troops.ai

"As a Founder, CEO, and angel investor, I am always thinking of ways to help companies grow. This book explains so much of what is missing in many sales environments and what change is necessary with the coming wave of machine learning and artificial intelligence."

—Tikhon Bernstam,
Founder & CEO, Parse & Scribd

"It's hard to believe that *Authentic Selling* is Jeff's first book, as he writes with both passion for the subject matter and maturity in its structure and form. But what struck me most about the book is that Jeff's belief that Authentic Selling is the best way to achieve success at this craft was completely validated by his own authenticity in presenting his arguments. With thousands of books on selling available to readers, it is Jeff's vulnerability and authenticity in presenting his own journey in sales that makes this work a standout. I highly recommend this book to both New and Veteran Sales Executives."

—Bob Almond, COO,
Full Armor Corporation

"Jeff does a great job of marrying tactical day to day examples of what sales leaders are dealing with, with analogies that help sellers understand the world they are living in. He provides meaningful go-forward advice for sales leaders at companies of all sizes. *Authentic Selling* is a fun, informative, and valuable read for anyone in sales."

—Henry Schuck, CEO,
Zoominfo

"Running a company at the intersection of personalization and automation, I know firsthand how important authenticity has become for the modern day sales pro. This is a great read for anyone serious about sales or even those who just want to understand basic, invaluable principles of selling."

—Kyle Porter, CEO,
SalesLoft

AUTHENTIC SELLING

How to Use the Principles of Sales
in Everyday Life

JEFF KIRCHICK

Much Will Be Expected LLC

Authentic Selling: How to Use the Principles of Sales in Everyday Life

Jeff Kirchick

Much Will Be Expected LLC
Published by Much Will Be Expected LLC
Copyright © 2020 by Jeff Kirchick

All rights reserved.

Much Will Be Expected LLC
41 Seaview Terrace, Chatham, MA 02633
Email: MuchWillBeExpected@gmail.com

Limit of Liability/Disclaimer of Warranty:

Publishing and editorial team: Author Bridge Media,
www.AuthorBridgeMedia.com
Project Manager and Editorial Director: Helen Chang
Publishing Manager: Laurie Aranda
Illustrations: Sam Espinosa

Library of Congress Control Number: 2020922044

ISBN 978-1-7359569-0-9—softcover
978-1-7359569-2-3—hardcover
978-1-7359569-1-6—Kindle
978-1-7359569-3-0—audiobook

Ordering Information:
Quantity sales. Special discounts are available on quantity purchases by corporations, associations, and others. For details, contact the publisher at the address above.

Printed in the United States of America

To my grandfather,
who never apologized for being himself.

Table of Contents

ACKNOWLEDGEMENTS

I have known for a long time that deep down, my passion is to write. My passion is to write because there is something therapeutic about getting things off your chest. But even more so, there is something special about touching peoples' lives through the written word. The biggest rush I get is writing something and getting positive feedback on it.

I think this desire to touch peoples' lives comes from my parents. From a young age, they taught me the importance of hard work and doing something meaningful with your life. I can never repay them for all that they did for me. I played sports every season from the time I was very young all the way through high school and even parts of college, and they never missed a game. They have always been my biggest cheerleaders, and they taught me the most valuable lessons I could ever know. This book would not be possible without them.

I also want to thank the amazing team I have worked with at Next Caller over the last seven years. The bulk of what I have learned about selling has come through my experience there and through the professional development opportunities afforded to me by the company. Specifically, I want to thank my boss, Ian Roncoroni, and fellow members of the leadership team, Tim Prugar and Sam Espinosa, who are some of my closest friends and supporters. I also want to thank the members of my team who inspire me every day to be the best leader that I can be.

Thank you to Julianne for always, always supporting me and listening to me. Thank you to my older brother, Jamie, who paved the way for me as a writer within the family. To my mentor, Bob Almond, thank you for keeping me in check and making sure I do not do anything stupid. And thank you to all those who read my manuscripts and gave me advice on how to best voice my opinions. Thank you to little Zoe, whose undying need for attention as I typed away at this made me take some necessary breaks.

Lastly, a special thank you to anyone I have crossed paths with who did not give me the benefit of the doubt. Without you to use as motivation, I would not be where I am today.

And of course, to you, the reader: thank you for coming on this journey with me.

FOREWORD

The goal for this book is pretty ambitious. I say that because I am trying to take a fairly focused topic—my selling philosophy—and seeing if I can make it matter to everyone. This book is not just for people who work in sales who want to pick up some new tips and tricks. This book is also for anyone who does not already realize that their entire life is made up of small moments where you are constantly negotiating on your own behalf. Understanding the principles that are shared in this book can be immensely valuable for anyone who wants to get more out of life. The best place to start is in your own interactions with other people.

Who am I and how do you know that this is worth reading? Well, you will determine that for yourself. I am currently a VP of Sales for an emerging tech company and I have had over a decade of successful selling experience. What I have enjoyed the most during that time is the relationships I have built with my customers. I always felt grateful to each and every one of them and sincerely wanted to do good by them for putting their faith in me. I started to notice a trend that customers could sense this passion. I felt compelled to write this book because so many sales programs today advise us to say and think things we would not authentically feel, and I feel that such a mindset is increasingly dangerous. I say it is an increasingly dangerous mindset because the coming wave of Artificial Intelligence will allow machines to learn the same programs that humans learn, and our authenticity is all we have then to distinguish us from the robots. It is high time to embrace who we are.

So, let's embrace who we are. Let's get weird.

Chapter 1

The Human Element of Sales

About a decade ago, I went in for a final round interview for a sales role at a firm in Boston. They decided for the last step to bring in the CEO to meet with me. I was probably no more than 24 years old and had been having a successful beginning to my sales career for a company right down the street. I will never forget my interview with the CEO, whose mission it seemed to be to belittle me and put me down from the moment he walked in the door. At the end of our interview, he told me that I was too cerebral for the job. He had based that upon my Princeton education, my private high school education—where his kids happened to have been students as well—and my interest in creative writing. I was too "all over the place" and interested in too many different things to possibly be successful in sales, because to be successful, I was going to need to be pigeon-holed into their sales training program. He told me verbatim, "I would rather hire a simpleton who graduated from [redacted] University who is not very smart but all he has in his life is pounding the phones for me eight hours a day and then slugging beers with his friends after work." I am not making up that quote—he really said that. I have had a chip on my shoulder ever since, and the successes I have had since that interview which include the publishing of this book are the proof that you should not judge people based on where they went to school, what they like to do in their free time, or how many beers they might slug after work every day. I can actually slug more beers in one sitting than that guy probably expected, for what it's worth, but it's beside the point: he was telling me that you need to be a certain type of person to be successful in sales. Ever since then, I have sought to prove him wrong: being your authentic self matters most in sales.

At that time, just a couple of years into my sales career back in 2012, I had built the most profitable vertical in my company. I had built a niche in my industry through social media, speaking opportunities, and writing for major publications as a young guy who was trying to predict the future about location-based social media. My prediction at the time was that social applications like Foursquare would lose their luster and cede market share to location-based applications that were more practical: ride-sharing (Uber), dating (Tinder), reviews (Yelp), and more. Since then, I joined Next Caller as one of its first employees. Next Caller got into Y-Combinator, a tech accelerator program that has also seen the likes of Airbnb, Dropbox, and Reddit. I have spent the last seven years selling multi-million dollar contracts to Fortune 500 brands looking to improve their customer experience while reducing fraud in their contact centers. But my education about sales started much earlier, perhaps even before I had set up a lemonade stand in my parents' driveway, peddling lemonade to passersby for pocket change.

From the day we are able to begin communicating and under-standing concepts, we begin our careers in sales and we begin a life of being sold to. Yes, your parents are salespeople, your siblings are salespeople, and you, too, have been a salesperson. Just because your family didn't have a leaderboard or a President's Club for its top performers does not make it any less true.

How is it possible that throughout your entire life these wolves have been hiding in sheep's clothing?

When you were a child, you were sold on a concept that eating your vegetables was good for you. You might have been sold on the idea that drinking milk would make you strong. Perhaps you were told that you could have dessert if you had your broccoli. Or that you could not see your friends until you completed your homework.

In school, your friends might have sold you on an idea to

play a certain game at recess. Or maybe as you got older, you were sold on trying a cigarette, a beer, or marijuana. If you were fortunate enough to go to college, keep in mind that various colleges competed for your tuition dollars, and many of them did so without even getting an opportunity to be on your radar, since their marketing dollars went to billboard advertisements or airport ads that you never saw.

After college, a job recruiter sells you on joining their company. In your personal life, you might find suitors trying to sell you on the idea that they are your perfect match. Not to mention that in plain sight up until this point there have been plenty of advertisements you heard on the radio or on television or that you just saw in passing while attending a sporting event at a stadium covered in brand logos. Various resources online suggest that the average individual is exposed to between 5,000 to 10,000 advertisements a day.

I could go on and on, but you get the picture. Although certainly, the same is also true in reverse.

When you were being sold on the idea of eating vegetables, you might have negotiated for yourself that you would eat your vegetables if it meant you got dessert. Perhaps you spent some of your free time trying to convince your parents to get you ice cream or cake. When you saw your friends at school, maybe part of the bargain for smoking a cigarette was that they would stop applying peer pressure. And again, perhaps you went on the offensive and tried to sell your friends on doing the things that you wanted to do: go to the movies, the mall, the beach. And when someone was trying to become your suitor, if you liked them back, you almost certainly tried to sell them on you—the same way you sold yourself to that job recruiter so that you could get the job you wanted.

What is true in almost all of these scenarios is that most people enter these situations without acknowledging the role of psychology, and specifically, the psychology of selling. There are few toddlers, for example, who have versed themselves in Sandler training (a formal sales training program) when they negotiate for themselves. Instead, they might resort to less professional tactics: crying, kicking, screaming, yelling, demanding, and just throwing a fit. And while that tactic might work on a tired parent who just wants to get on with things, it rarely (if ever) works when the stakes are raised.

Here is something to consider about all of these sales interactions you have had throughout your life: How many times were you lied to so that someone else could get their way? I am in relatively good shape, but all that milk I drank did not lead to any big growth spurts. I was also told that eating my spinach would make me big and strong like Popeye.

Have you been in a relationship where you found out later that someone you trusted had not been forthcoming with you about something? Have you bought a product that was advertised on TV and found out that the real thing paled in comparison? Did your older brother or sister ever promise you that you could ride in the front seat of the car on the way back from wherever you were going, but then slammed the door in your face when the time of reckoning came?

Now you have an understanding that your entire life has been a constant back and forth of selling people on things that you want for yourself or even things that you want for them while being sold to by the same people. And we know that most of the people you interact with throughout your life are not trained salespeople and that they go about their acts of persuasion in dubious ways that often overlook what *you* want. What naturally happens to a person's psyche when—throughout their entire life—they are often lied to about exactly what it is that is going to happen if they say "Yes?"

Or, if we take it down a notch, what happens when many people throughout your life do not lie to you, but never ask you the questions they should be asking to make a proper recommendation since they lack the proper sales fundamentals, most notably an empathic mindset?

If time and time again you are sold on an idea throughout your life and you end up with something less than what you expected, naturally you will start to mistrust these salespeople. This is most evident in more overt sales settings, like a car dealership. But is that used car salesperson really any different than anyone else in your life who encouraged you to do something, or are they just the manifestation in your mind of what an untrustworthy individual ought to look like simply because your less conscious experiences with salespeople have been imperfect?

A couple things happen as a result of the disappointment you have felt. First, you become hyper-aware of when someone is selling you something. You might not have considered your college search a sales process and you might never have looked at the college admissions counselors as salespeople, but you certainly look at the used car salesperson as a sales representative when you walk onto the lot to buy a car. How you act in the latter scenario is likely to be a little different than when you walk into

the admissions office, in large part because there is an aware-
ness that exists in the latter scenario that may not exist in the
former.

Second, consciously or subconsciously, you may start to
put your guard up over time. Sure, when you were a kid, you
did not have much of a choice but to eat your vegetables. You
probably questioned things less than you do today. But as time
goes on and your sensitivity grows to possibly being let down,
you ask more questions. What exactly are these vegetables doing
that I cannot get from a multi-vitamin? Is my mother actually
concerned about my vegetable intake, or at this point is she
just trying to make sure I am doing OK in my life? Well, I
suppose if you are an adult and you are reading this, the hope
would be that your mother is not still bearing on you to eat those
veggies.

Now, to be sure, there are many times you are sold on doing
something and you are grateful for it. In fact, I would hope that
this is true the overwhelming majority of the time. The veggies
you were advised to eat probably did not kill you; if they had,
you would not be reading this book. The college you were sold
on attending might have been the best four years of your life.
The job you were sold on taking or the spouse you were sold on
accepting into your life might have been the best things that ever
happened to you. Ideally, your life is one where more often than
not, the things you were promised turned out to be everything
you hoped for and then some.

This doesn't change the very real likelihood that you still had
enough negative outcomes over the course of your life to at least
question things before taking action. In other words, it's nearly

impossible that every single outcome has been positive for you, enough so that you would just blindly follow any advice that anyone gives you. That would be insane, especially considering the diversity of thought and opinion on this planet. If you blindly pursued any action anyone advised you to take, you would be facing some consequences the moment you ran into someone who disagreed with something you said.

When we have had enough of these "bad" experiences, we begin to question things. And ultimately what helps us negotiate with the world is the authenticity we feel in the person who is selling us.

Think about it: if you had good parents, they presented their ideas with authenticity. They would tell you that they love you and that they have your best interests at heart. Part of their pitch would include that they were once a child like you and therefore they know the ropes on what it takes to become successful, healthy adults like them. If they were good parents, you likely felt and knew that they loved you without them needing to include that in their sales pitch. And that feeling—that you are loved and that the other person is looking out for you—is what authenticity is all about.

There are a lot of sales training programs out there that teach you how to sell. And to be sure, there are nuggets, bits, and pieces in most of these programs that are valuable. Indeed, I have found advice to be helpful from a wide array of these programs, as well as from various thought leaders, consultants, and mentors with whom I have spoken. But by and large, I think any program that trains you to say and do things that are a departure from the way you would interact with your family or your best friend are mostly a waste of time. While this viewpoint may be controversial, I think there are compelling reasons to completely re-think the way we feel about selling.

Why is that? Well, first and foremost, I just gave you the answer. Authenticity shines when human beings are otherwise accustomed to being suspicious or worried about being let down. But this is more topical than ever in the age of Machine Learning (ML) and Artificial Intelligence (AI). I could joke about how some of these sales programs want to take people in, give them a formula, and spit them out as robots, but it is not really a joke any more. There has been a massive spike in how the sales world has embraced ML and AI, with virtual assistants that now send emails in cadences to prospects, voice recognition technology that picks up on the buzzwords that resonate with customers, and even bots on websites that can answer basic questions about a product. It used to be human beings who manually wrote all of their emails, took notes on all of their calls, and responded to inbound leads. There used to be entire teams dedicated to responding to inbound leads. Now it is commonplace for machines to be fulfilling the same responsibilities.

My point here is pretty simple: embracing an authentic sales strategy is imperative if you do not want to be replaced by a machine. Because the time is quickly approaching where companies can use ML, AI, and big data to program a machine with all the skills it needs to speak to a customer in the "perfect" way. Companies can take MEDICC or Sandler Training or BANT and program it into a machine. What companies cannot program into a machine is human nature. The only advantage that any of us have over the machine is our human nature. And what is unique about our human nature versus the formulaic and canned responses of the machine is our authenticity.

To be sure, some people reading this book may not be interested in a career in sales, and more interested in the general principles of sales and how to apply them to everyday life. That is perfectly fine, but I would still make two simple arguments.

First, the position I take above about robots replacing salespeople still holds true for our day-to-day lives. ML & AI are sweeping into every facet of our lives, not just the sales world. And if Netflix knows which documentary your girlfriend wants to watch next better than you do, or if her ex-boyfriend used algorithms to buy her perfect gifts because you never spent the time truly getting to know her, you might be in trouble. By being authentic, however, you might outsmart the AI.

We continue to see AI creating broad-sweeping change all over the world. In the run-up to the 2020 Presidential election, Democratic candidate Andrew Yang made a name for himself by discussing the dangers of automation and how we need to account for future job loss in industries like trucking, since autonomous, self-driving vehicles will erase the need for a human being to operate the vehicles. The same can be said with the innovation of Elon Musk at Tesla, whose experimentation with self-driving vehicles runs parallel to that of tech giants like Uber, which already has cars on the road that do not require a human driver. Our system of manned tollbooths has been replaced by EZ-Pass, which is now ubiquitous on our highways. So it is not a matter of if—it is simply a matter of when, and as I mentioned just a moment ago, the proliferation of this type of technology has already infiltrated the sales world en masse.

The second point is more important though, because it is not just the emergence of AI that makes authenticity more valuable. It is because our brains are highly capable of noticing trends and patterns throughout our lives. We constantly use data to make better decisions; in fact, we have a term for it: the feedback loop. When you touch a hot stove for the first time, you scream. Then, you probably never do it again for the rest of your life. The first time you get the wool pulled over your eyes by someone, you do a little post-mortem in your head about what happened. You get better and better about this over time. Long story short, you start to understand when you feel someone is being authentic and when someone is just full of it.

So, authentic selling is as good as it gets for two reasons:

1. The emergence and future improvement of ML and AI will commoditize all systems-based selling programs. This seems inevitable.
2. The human psyche is adept at identifying when someone is being their authentic self through trial and trauma.

But what does it even mean to engage in authentic selling?

Chapter 2

What is Authentic Selling?

Required reading for any salespeople that I hire is a book called *The Humble Inquiry* by Edgar Schein. The book is about asking questions instead of telling people things. And the word "humble" is there purposefully, because it denotes the humility of the person asking the questions. The asker of the questions does not pretend to know the answers. The person asking the questions has no agenda. The person asking the questions puts themselves in almost a subservient position by asking the questions rather than by telling. The power is shifted to the individual providing the answers. Most importantly, the person asking the questions is genuinely interested in the answers and does not ask the questions for question's sake.

On Day 1 of training for my new sales hires, I ask them what they think is the most important skill to have in sales. No one ever gets the question right. The answers vary, and I can walk you through some of the wrong answers and why they are wrong before we get to the right answer.

One common answer is that you need to be "personable" or "charming" to be in sales. It certainly does not hurt to be personable. A lot of people imagine salespeople as being very outgoing. Client entertainment is a very real thing, and a good salesperson might have to be good at taking a customer out on the town, wining and dining them, and telling jokes along the way.

I'll explain why this is nearly meaningless with a simple question. If you had a newborn baby, would you trust that outgoing sales weasel who took you out for a fun night in Vegas to babysit him or her for you? The answer is probably not. But even if your best friend (or parent) is the most boring person in the world, you would probably prefer to have either of them do the babysitting instead if those were your only options. Why is that? Because you know and trust your best friend or your parent, and the outgoing sales weasel—though he or she may be quite funny and affable—is not someone that you truly know and trust. They are just someone that you like.

My uncle founded an event over thirty years ago called the "Matzo Ball." It was actually a very good idea. Realizing that Jewish singles had nothing to do on Christmas Eve except eat Chinese food, he organized a Jewish singles party nationwide on December 24th. The event was wildly successful and it is still an annual event. I spent many years in my childhood working the cash register with my brother, my parents, and my grandparents. Normally, nightclubs have an attractive young person collecting money at the front, not a kid with his Gameboy and two generations of family members. This was because my uncle trusted us not to steal any of the cash from him. This is a good example of how trust supersedes personality and affability.

Another common response that I receive is "presentation skills." Again, it's not a bad answer. The problem with this answer is that it assumes that what you are presenting to the customer is something that they need. What if your company does 1,000 things and your customer only needs a handful of those things? You could have the best presentation skills in the world, but if you are spending most of your time presenting concepts that are not going to land with the customer, then all you really have is a wasted skill.

Yet another response I get is "persistence" or "perseverance." These are indeed crucial aspects to being successful in any sales environment. The problem is that these are skills that are crucial to succeed in most all aspects of life, unless you have been granted the gift of the silver spoon. Very few of us never need to persevere to earn what we want in our lives. It should be no different in sales.

Where people get a little bit warmer is when they say "communication skills." This answer is vague enough that it kind of encompasses the right answer, which I am going to get to in a moment. To be sure, communication skills are pretty important in the sales world. There is a level of patience, understanding, and ability to articulate concepts clearly which goes a long way. The thing is, in the absence of the most important skill for selling, you could have the absolute best communication skills and still lose out to someone else with poorer communication skills, simply because they possess the one skill that matters most.

I could go on and on, but hopefully the first paragraph of the chapter gave away that the answer is "Listening." Listening is the most important skill in sales. Anyone who says otherwise, I would love to listen to what they have to say rather than tell them why I think they are wrong.

See what I did there?

You cannot sell anything to anyone unless you understand what it is that they actually need. Too many people go into sales presentations with an agenda. They have a belief that the customer needs their product and that they need it right now without ever having had a conversation with them. Imagine how you feel when someone has the utmost conviction for you to do something that you absolutely know you do not want to do. How insulting is it to you that the other person acts like they know what is best for you without even consulting you to get your perspective? What is your visceral reaction to the phrase, "You need this," versus your visceral reaction to the phrase "What do you need?"

The former statement makes assumptions. It is a telling attitude. I am telling you that you need this thing. When you tell people how to think, you are taking away their agency. However, when you ask someone what they need, you are doing the exact opposite. You are empowering that person. You are entrusting them with the ability to decide for themselves what they think they need. You are acknowledging to them that you are coming from a place of inexperience and that you are seeking to understand.

It is difficult to tell people what to do and to be authentic about wanting what is best for them. When you tell people what to do, you are doing what is best for you. When you ask people what they need, you are being authentic—as long as you really care. Surely at some point when you were a child, you cried for some reason. Hopefully, your mom or dad asked you, "What's wrong?" rather than saying, "Shut up."

Imagine a hypothetical scenario where someone comes home from work and finds that their partner is making dinner. They ask their partner, "What time will dinner be ready?" Their partner responds, "You have time to take a nap."

You might be thinking to yourself that the partner was not listening. After all, the question asked was when dinner would be ready. The answer received was fairly open-ended and did not seem to address the question. But what was really being asked?

It is through listening and asking questions that we understand the true motivations of an individual. In this scenario, this individual and their partner probably have some sort of underlying context from their relationship which causes the partner to respond this way. The partner knows that the other person comes home from work tired every day and is eager to take a nap. What is unclear is whether or not they have time to take a nap. In that sense, you could argue that the partner is actually a very good listener, because the partner understands why the question is being asked and knows what the real answer is to the question.

In the consulting world, there is a phenomenon known as the five "why's." The general premise is that you need to ask someone "Why?" five times in order to really get to the root of anything.

Something I ask everyone I hire is "Why do you get out of bed every day to do what you do?" or, more succinctly, "What is your 'Why'?". The answers I have received have varied tremendously and oftentimes I am very surprised. I say I am surprised because sometimes it really only takes one "Why" to get the answer I am looking for. But usually that is not the case.

If I told you that my "Why" is to make as much money as I possibly can, you would likely have a perception that I am greedy, driven by money, and lack concern for my fellow man. You might even assume my political affiliation and believe I am incredibly fond of capitalism. But if you prodded me and asked "Why do you want to make a lot of money?", my answer might surprise you.

If I then turned around and told you that writing is my greatest passion and that I want to have financial freedom so that I could pursue a career in the arts or writing, you might feel embarrassed for having judged me so harshly just a moment ago. In fact, you might be grateful that you asked the question for fear of having unjustly and unnecessarily written me off. Now, your curiosity might be building, so you might ask me "Why?" once more.

At that point, I might tell you that writing is cathartic for me. It helps me get things off my chest. I might also tell you that I think there is a special power in being able to move others. Now, we have come quite a long way from where we started—which was something to do with making a lot of money. Naturally, you ask me "Why" once more.

At this point, I might tell you that I have been very fortunate in my life. I grew up in an upper middle-class family who supported me emotionally and financially through one of the elite all-boys' private high schools in Boston and a college education at Princeton University. My high school had a motto, "From those to whom much has been given, much will be expected." Perhaps I tell you that I feel a sense of responsibility to give back to others, and that I think I can give back to the world by sharing my knowledge through writing.

This seems like a noble cause, but you have only asked me "Why" four times, and I just told you that it can take five tries. So you ask me "Why" one final time.

This time, I tell you that bringing joy to others has always brought me more joy than anything I could possibly do for myself.

Now, think about how far we have come in this entire exercise. We started out with what was probably the most utterly self-interested and materialistic answer possible: "I care about making money." But over the course of asking "Why?" we got to the exact opposite extreme: "I care about helping other people be happy."

When you have an agenda in your interactions with others, you do not allow yourself the opportunity to get to the bottom of things. You assume what is best for others and you take what they say at face value. Having an agenda makes you less likely to want to listen to someone else. It also makes you see their responses through the lens of your own agenda. Think about times you have argued with someone over politics, or really anything for that matter. You probably find yourself sometimes itching for the other person to stop talking so that you can tell them why they are wrong. This makes you less likely to really listen to what they are saying, to take it all in, and to form an honest opinion. When you have an agenda, you are more interested in being right than you are interested in being a listener.

Now that we understand the power of listening, we should differentiate between active listening and listening for listening's sake. Just because you listen and ask questions does not mean that you do so with a genuine desire to help someone. The most obvious example of a question with an agenda would be something like, "Wouldn't buying our product solve your problems?" This question is really more of a statement, and it's an "us" statement, not a "them" statement. When I say that, I mean that it is a question driven by our own agenda to sell our product, not genuinely focused on solving a problem for the customer.

I recently got a cold call from a sales rep who was trying to sell me sales enablement technology for my sales team. I politely told the rep that whatever he was selling was not of interest to me. He asked a follow up question, "So are you not interested in driving as much revenue as you possibly can for your team?" Questions like these are so dumb and inauthentic that they immediately turn me off, and I assume they turn off most people. No one asks these types of questions unless they have an agenda. Of course, in my job as a VP of Sales for a technology company, I care about driving as much revenue as I possibly can. The individual on the other end of the line clearly had a script he was reading off of to corner me into agreeing that his product was useful. Two things can be true at once: I can be interested in doing the best job I can, and I can believe that certain products will not help me in that effort. When people ask questions that are obviously designed to be manipulative traps, most common-sense people know what is going on and become even less obliged to continue the conversation.

I went in reverse and said "No, I do not care about that." The sales rep seemed shocked and repeated the question to me, "You don't care about driving as much revenue as you can?" to which I replied, "That's correct." The conversation ended quickly.

A better approach would have been to have delivered an open-ended question, something like this:

"What matters to you the most right now in your role as a VP of Sales?"

Through getting to know me, it is actually quite likely that the sales rep would have been able to get through to me with whatever they were selling. But by coming in with an agenda and asking questions that feel inauthentic to any listener, he ruined his opportunity to even get far enough into the conversation with me.

Think about times in your life when you wanted something for yourself versus times in your life when you helped someone you care about. When your parent or sibling, your best friend or your spouse, boyfriend, or girlfriend complains to you about something, hopefully you seek to understand what is going on in a meaningful way, diagnose the issue, and help them find a solution that works for them. When you want something for yourself, you might find yourself bargaining with people or telling them what you want and why you want it. There is an absolutely noticeable difference in these interactions.

Let's take a real-world example.

Let's say a close family member comes to you because they are having an issue at work and they are seeking your advice. In this scenario, because your family member is dear to you, you are eager to listen and help because you have a personal vested interest in their well-being and happiness. You listen carefully as they explain the situation to you. You might even have several follow-up questions so that you can contextualize the situation. Why? Because you want to give the best advice possible, and you can only do that if you have all of the facts. In this scenario, you have nothing really to gain but a feeling of pride in helping someone that you care about. By the end of the conversation, you have given your feedback, your family member thanks you, and you both continue about your day.

But what if the roles were reversed and it was you going to someone close to you for help? Going into that conversation, you might actually be hoping to get a certain answer from that individual, so you merely use them as a backdrop upon which you can go forward with some foregone conclusion of yours. You might even influence their advice by providing certain facts in favor of your idea while omitting facts that work against the conclusions you are hoping to reach together. That is because your ego has taken over. You are no longer an objective recipient of information; instead, you are driving forward a personal agenda.

But there is also something to be said for the way we are naturally inclined to help people we know and trust versus those that we do not. Think about social media interactions, for example. How many times do you see acquaintances arguing about politics on Facebook, where the conversations quickly devolve into ad hominem attacks? Any question, for example, that starts with "How could you..." is not a question that seeks to understand; it is instead the type of question you ask when you are incredulous that someone could hold a certain position. When someone says "How could you vote for that person?", they are not actually interested in your answer—they are interested in condemning you for your personal choices. People get so worked up in these conversations—they feel their heart race and blood rushes to their brains as they get so infuriated that another human being could have such a vile opinion.

When someone you are close with similarly expresses an opinion you disagree with, chances are that you will not rush to call them names. Nothing else has changed, though. You might still be surprised by their perspective, especially because they are such a close friend to you, and you might have expected them to share more of your viewpoints. But what happens in this latter scenario if the person is truly close to you is that you actually are more likely to become curious than concerned. After all, you trust your closest advisers and friends. If they start espousing a viewpoint that is unfamiliar to you, you are more likely to give the benefit of the doubt.

What has truly changed in both scenarios? We have a tendency to involve our ego and our agenda when there is less at stake in doing so. There is a natural deference of our ego to people we really like and respect because we value their input and their seat at the table. But with an acquaintance voicing a political opinion you disagree with you may be less apt to ask questions or seek to understand. This is something you would be unlikely to do to your best friend, however, or even your close family member. Our ego has a propensity to take control more often with people for whom we care less about; we are naturally more inclined to want to listen to the people that we do really care about. And that is because we are more inclined to give the benefit of the doubt to people whom we find authentic and whom we trust—even if they sometimes drive us crazy. We know they will have our backs when we need them to and we have their backs when they need us, so we listen closely to them whereas we are much faster to write off other people.

Now, of course I realize that people get angry at their close friends and family members all the time on social media. There are exceptions to any rule of course, but there is still an important difference in the examples that I just gave. In the first example, the issue you are consulted about feels like it has nothing to do with you, but obviously it is much more important to you, since it involves someone close to you. In the latter example, whatever debate is happening online does not involve you either, and the table stakes are certainly lower, because you are not even being addressed for feedback anyhow. But what happens in that latter scenario is that your ego is activated. Your mind has a way of telling you that this is personal even when it is not. And when you act out of selfish interest—an interest in making sure you tell everyone you are right and they are wrong—you are inherently starting from a place where it will be difficult to exhibit empathy.

With your close friend, your ego is not activated because you feel comfortable with them and you value that they have consulted you to begin with.

In order to engage in Authentic Selling, you probably need to sell a vision that is broader than the thing you are actually trying to sell. Think about it: when you are helping a friend or family member with an issue, you have no agenda other than helping them. That means that you might offer them a variety of ideas as part of an overall solution. Now, if someone approached me about getting some sales tips, I could tell them to go buy this book on Amazon.com. And maybe the book would help them. But it would unmistakably be a sales pitch if that was my only answer for them, and it would feel like I just have an agenda to push my book on people. If instead I asked them why they needed the help, I would start to uncover some more granular data points. Perhaps it is evident to me now that I need to make recommendations about professional development organizations, mentorship ideas, books (mine or others possibly included), and different types of practice. When I have suggested all these ideas, I am selling the individual on the bigger picture. This is a big hit to the ego, but the reality is, really nobody sells a product that single-handedly makes someone else's life perfect. Whatever you are selling—professionally or personally—is just solving a particular problem right now. I do not think it would be controversial to state that people get more excited when more of their problems are being solved at once. When you sell the bigger picture—which means consulting the customer beyond pitching your own product—you are accomplishing two things. First, you are just helping them a lot more than you would be otherwise.

Second—and more importantly—you are acting authentically, the same way you would treat a friend, for whom you have no agenda whatsoever other than their well-being.

Most traditional sales programs do not engage in Authentic Selling. They fundamentally cannot, because the very idea of having a "philosophy" on how to behave requires someone to behave differently than what their natural inclinations might otherwise dictate for them. Let's just think about this simply from the top down in most organizations.

The CEO reports to the board, and the board has ambitious goals for the company this year. So the CEO sits down with the company's revenue leader and explains the ambitious goals and what kind of growth needs to be attained over time. In turn, the revenue leader sits down with her army of salespeople and explains the goals to them. But she knows all the while that she needs to have insight into what is going on within her ranks so that she can properly report to the CEO and the board, so she feels forced to lose her own authenticity in how she might want to manage her team and instead resorts to measures that she knows will help her look good to the CEO and the board. What are those measures?

First and foremost, she implements a quota for all of her reps. This ensures that they will work hard towards a goal and be compensated based upon their ability to drive revenue for the company and their ability to march the sales team towards its common revenue goal. This will make it easy for her to know who on the team is going to help carry them to the goal and who will need to be replaced by other, more worthy sales reps. What is lost in all of this is a lack of trust and autonomy for the team members. Surely, you would never tell one of your friends that you have a "quota" for them, and that if you do not have fun hanging out with them more than three times in one calendar year, that you might consider replacing them with another friend. More importantly, the revenue leader has overlooked the very real possibility that her team of sales reps will now inevitably change their behavior towards customers based on how they are pacing against quota and what time of the month it is. If you have never been on the receiving end of a sales interaction where the sales rep is desperately looking to meet quota, then good for you. It is not fun to be a customer in that situation most of the time. I have even had sales reps tell me not to interact with other sales reps in their own company for fear of missing their own personal quotas!

What else happens? The revenue leader needs to be able to forecast properly so that she knows how to set expectations for the CEO and the board. And in order to forecast properly, she needs to make sure that certain questions get answered whenever a sales rep is talking to a prospect. She might even deploy the famous "BANT" model, which stands for "Budget, Authority, Need, Timing." This model suggests that a lead is not qualified unless the prospect has the budget for a project, authority to make a decision, a need for the product being sold, and an ability to move forward quickly. What happens when the reps get on the phone with new prospects? They literally ask the prospect these questions. Do you have budget? Are you the decision-maker? Do you need our product? Can you move forward quickly?

These questions are not rooted in an interest in the prospect. They are rooted in self-interest. And that is what makes them fundamentally problematic. If you are on the receiving end of a sale and getting questions about your budget and whether or not you are the decision-maker, it feels like the sales rep is interested in figuring out whether or not they can generate a sale. If you had some conflict with a friend because their significant other was keeping them from doing something with you, it would probably not be a good idea to ask your friend whether they make the decisions for themselves or if their significant other is the decision-maker in the relationship. Even if you were interested in the answer, you would know not to ask such a question because it would surely be considered offensive or rude.

What other traps does the revenue leader set for her team that prevent them from being their authentic selves? Well, by default, the revenue leader's job is to be data-driven, so she must mandate that her team fill out certain information about every conversation they have so that the data can be used for strategic decision-making at the leadership level. It might be as simple as trying to understand something like the percentage of customers who are already working with or speaking with a competitor. Knowing such a statistic would be useful for understanding whether or not the presentation materials should speak to competitive differentiation against competitors, or if it should focus exclusively on how the product itself solves a problem. Perhaps the revenue leader wants to measure what percentage of the time the company is talking to an actual decision-maker. This would necessitate her to mandate that sales reps ask their prospects point blank, "Are you the decision maker?"

Inevitably, this does cause some problems. Because if it is mandated that a sales rep needs to know whether or not the prospect is using or speaking with a competitor, time that could have been spent having authentic conversation is instead spent running through a script that was pre-ordained by the revenue leader. And to the point I made earlier, the more and more that sales becomes scripted, the less and less we will need human beings for the job. And that is a bad outcome for the sales professionals who are reading this book, as well as for the everyday people who are looking to learn about applying sales strategies into their everyday lives.

I want to be clear in that I am not against compiling data for strategic reasons, nor am I against asking good questions that inform whether or not a prospect is qualified. I am just against asking for the wrong reasons. What I have found to be the case is that generally prospects will open up about the information that sales leaders want to know about if they feel that you deserve to know that information. For example, if you are going to embark on a proof-of-concept with a prospect, it stands to reason that you have earned the right to understand what their process is for purchasing your product, because certainly you are not going to go through with doing all the work for a proof-of-concept without ensuring that there is a path forward for you and the customer. Most reasonable customers will see things this way. And that is really no different than being in a relationship. You might not ask on the first date whether or not the other person is going to be intimate with you, let alone marry you someday. But as you continue dating, you both earn a right to ask one another if this relationship actually has a chance of going somewhere. Odds are slim you would even get that far though if you did indeed ask about having sex the moment you met. That is a turnoff, much like it is a turnoff to ask a prospect if they are ready to buy from you during your first phone call. Obviously, there are some exceptions, but you get my point.

The moral of the story is that sales leaders with agendas are capable of making their salespeople have agendas, and I think that this is bad. It is really no different from everyday life. Growing up, you might want certain things for yourself, but the desires of your parents or friends might steer you in a different direction. They have their own agendas and sometimes their agenda involves you doing things you would not be naturally inclined to do on your own. Today, when we turn on our televisions, we succumb to the respective agendas of the media. On one hand, CNN has an agenda, and on the other, so does Fox News. I have experimented with flipping between both channels when they are reporting on the same piece of 'news', and it is remarkable to note how perfectly capable they both are of ignoring certain facts that do not suit their agenda, all for the purpose of allowing their agenda to influence what yours ought to be.

Earlier in this chapter, I gave two different examples: a family member who comes to you for advice versus you going to them for advice, and the difference between how you might treat friends versus acquaintances on social media or for political leanings in general. There are really two points to be made. One is that we are our best selves when we have no agenda whatsoever. The second is that we are much more likely to treat our close friends better than our acquaintances.

In the first scenario where you are being asked for advice, you avoid injection of your ego as much as you reasonably can because you care about the well-being of your friend. In the second scenario where an acquaintance ticks you off by saying something you do not like, you are more likely to embrace your ego and assert your own agenda so that you can feel good about yourself. The reason you are likely to behave this way is because you are naturally more willing to extend the benefit of the doubt to people that you know and trust. There are exceptions to this rule and you may find yourself losing your patience with close friends or family on social media from time to time. Presumably though you will have a higher tolerance threshold for those people than you have for your acquaintances.

So, with that in mind, what is Authentic Selling, defined?

Authentic Selling is treating an individual like they are a close friend. Authentic Selling is treating someone as if they are within your "Circle of Trust." Authentic Selling is behaving the way you behave when your close family member seeks your guidance. Authentic Selling is being your authentic self as a result of the comfort you feel in natural dialogue with someone whom you trust. And in order to be good at being authentic, it is important to learn how to have empathy.

Chapter 3

On Empathy

Part I

Good news and bad news. The bad news is that this chapter is a
little heavy on politics. The good news is that you will not find
that topic much elsewhere throughout the book. But I warned
you at the beginning that this book is about applying the principles of sales to everyday life. And never in my lifetime have

politics seemed more a part of our everyday lives than now. Understanding how to deal with people who disagree with you can be a matter of preserving your friendships (and your sanity); you will even need to understand how to deal with people who write you off completely over such disagreement.

I begin by mentioning that politically speaking, I am pretty much in the center. If you are opinionated one way or the other and cannot fathom how anyone could refuse to place themselves on either the right or the left, consider finishing the chapter on empathy before you put the book away.

As a centrist, I am naturally used to having people disagree with me about things, whether left-leaning or right-leaning people. Either way, people are going to disagree with you no matter what opinions you have and you need to be able to understand how to handle those situations. It is no secret that the media, cable news especially, makes their money by creating outrage, and that social media companies benefit from it as well. It should be no surprise also that polarization in our country is at an all-time high, with more people than ever firmly entrenched in their camps, Team Red or Team Blue, unable to really think for themselves any more on an issue-by-issue basis. If you turn on CNN or MSNBC, liberal news anchors attempt to discredit their conservative peers by assuming what their intentions must be in holding certain policy positions. When you turn on Fox News, their anchors do the same exact thing in reverse. It becomes difficult who to believe.

In today's political climate, there is a lot of noise within which everything seems to exist except empathy. I found myself caring more about empathy in recent years because my Achilles Heel is that I wear my heart on my sleeve. I wanted to be better about the way I respond to situations—positive or negative—by putting my immediate emotional reaction to something to the side and thinking about it more objectively. This was particularly true in workplace interactions where I wanted to improve my ability to negotiate with co-workers and prospects. As part of that ongoing effort, I began to work with a leadership coach. I explained to her that I wanted to improve in this area. She gave me a very simple piece of advice:

"People do not try to suck on purpose."

To be totally clear, I am not of the mindset that people suck, nor do I think that people are always wrong when they frustrate me or make me upset. Rather, when it appears that someone is acting in a frustrating manner, more often than not, they are not doing so purposefully. Or, to dig deeper, that there are circumstances unbeknownst to me surrounding the way they behave, which would otherwise make me more sympathetic to their behavior if only I had the full context.

Here is a real-world example. When I was younger, I considered myself politically progressive. Anchoring me to that mindset was the fact that my older brother is gay, and that gay rights were at the epicenter of political discussions at that moment. I was not a very political person otherwise, and because I felt that social issues dominated all other issues (e.g., the economy, healthcare, gun control, etc.), I felt righteous in my determination that anyone who disagreed with me must be a bigot. Never mind that my gay older brother was himself politically conservative—in my mind, he was wrong for siding with the enemy. See the irony in this: I had so much conviction in my own beliefs that I took away someone else's agency to form their own opinion on what was best for them.

At that time, I worked in a company and had a number of colleagues who were Mormons. They were very friendly people, but some of them posted things on Facebook that upset me. There were videos of people in LDS churches talking about how homosexuality was a sin. In my mind, I found their viewpoints hypocritical, especially in that they were picking and choosing certain things from the Bible to uphold while ignoring others. Even fundamental science as we know and understand it today is rejected in the Bible, so why were people so fixated on homosexuality? I jumped to the conclusion that my coworkers must have been purposeful in their intellectual inconsistency around their interpretation of the Bible and that they must just hate gay people. However, I am not sure that this conclusion was fair.

Here is what I mean about empathy, and it has little to do with the person I was back then. The person I was back then would write those people off as homophobic bigots. In fact, that is probably what I did at the time, even if I never said so to those people directly. But empathy is about putting yourself in someone else's shoes. If I was indoctrinated with the same message for my entire life, how am I to know that I would have the capacity to be better than the next person at taking in new information and putting it into action? To be clear, I am not condoning the viewpoint itself. I obviously still disagree with the message those people were sending. The question is whether to determine that they were hateful or if their perspective was affected for some other reason, like many years of their upbringing. Those are two very different things.

Here is another example. Personally, I am pro-choice. I always have been and that will probably never change. Generally, what I have found is that people who disagree with me do so either for religious reasons, or because they believe that terminating a prospective human life as it is developing in utero amounts to murder. But when I hear my fellow pro-choice advocates describe abortion opponents, it is as misogynists who use the issue of abortion as a justification for the oppression of women. While it is probable that some pro-life advocates do, in fact, overlook the autonomy of women in forming their opinion, I view these ideas as mutually exclusive. In other words, while I disagree with the pro-life stance, I accept the possibility that someone might disagree with me for what are wholly legitimate reasons to them, while recognizing and being empathetic to the disproportionate burden this places on women.

Let's go back to my leadership coach. She talked about how people do not try to suck on purpose. What this really means is that people do not wake up every day trying to be bad. I believe that. I find it unrealistic to accept that most people are not trying their best, whatever that best might look like. For some, it appears more obvious than it does for others. People who are perpetually late, for example, have trouble being organized. What if you learned that that individual has attention-deficit disorder? Someone cuts you off on your way to work. What if you learned that they were on the way to the hospital? I once got a speeding ticket as a teenager because I was late for work leaving the gravesite of a friend who had passed away. I tearfully explained the situation to the officer. "Well, your day just got worse," he told me. He was not empathetic. When I told that story to the judge, she waived the speeding ticket. She was more empathetic. But perhaps, look-ing back on it, I am being unfair to the officer. I don't know what he had been going through that day.

Part of cognitive-behavioral therapy is looking at specific sit-uations and outlining what possibilities exist beyond your initial reaction. When your co-worker is late in handing you something you asked for, you immediately think to yourself, "They do not value my time, clearly, and so they probably do not respect me." That is the immediate, emotional reaction. Acting upon that emotional reaction would be a huge mistake, because it jumps to a conclusion without firm evidence, while ignoring other plausi-ble possibilities.

An alternative possibility might be the exact opposite: your co-worker respects your hard work and effort so much that they put too much time into the project making sure they got it done perfectly, hoping it would help you out as much as possible. Or, maybe you did a poor job of communicating to your co-worker the magnitude of the project in the first place and they simply did not understand its importance. Another possibility is that all projects have been late by this individual because they are going through something at home, or because they are poorly organized and need some professional development help. The only answer that is generally clear at the outset is that you do not know the answer: you just have assumptions.

This is true today for nearly every part of our national dia-logue. With regard to the disagreements on the United States' southern border, liberals believe conservatives are hateful racists, while conservatives believe liberals are advocating for anarchy and open borders. In both cases, an assumption is made about what someone is really trying to say, and both times, it is generally untrue.

Here is a more nuanced approach. Perhaps, after all, both sides want a lot of the same things, if they would desist from generalizations about one another and establish some common language. Perhaps they both agree that people should be treated humanely. After all, even prisoners who have committed serious crimes in the United States are entitled to some basic privileges above and beyond what are given to animals. Perhaps they also agree that there should be uniform protocols for lawfully immigrating to the United States. Most likely, they agree that there needs to be a fair immigration system in place so that all immigrants are treated equally and fairly under the law. They likely both agree that having open borders is not a solution. Agreeing on these basic concepts establishes the foundation for a more productive dialogue, one which might otherwise avoid detouring on one side to comparisons of present conditions to Nazi concentration camps, and on the other side to the insistence that we chant the battle cry "Build the Wall!" which, intentional or not, gives a xenophobic vibe.

My interest in empathy spiked a few years ago when I started feeling more than ever that this quality was missing from conversations about everyday things. I recall my dismay at an article that more or less celebrated the death of a young American man, Otto Warmbier, who had traveled to North Korea and had been punished—according to the author—for flaunting his "white male privilege." To me, it felt entirely inappropriate to celebrate the death of anyone, regardless of whether or not their actions were reckless. It felt more likely to me that whatever hubris Warmbier felt in traveling to North Korea as a US citizen, that his death was still tragic and did not deserve to be turned into a lesson about race, for which there was no substantiating evidence anyhow. However, because the article was written by a Black woman, many accused me of being a racist simply for questioning her position. An alternative possibility did not exist in the mind of my accusers that perhaps I simply disagreed with the author and that it had nothing to do with my skin color or her skin color or gender. It certainly never crossed my mind to call my accuser an anti-Semite since Warmbier was Jewish, and that is because empathy generally should preclude people from making accusations about other people without compelling evidence. In this case, whatever evidence there was of wrongdoing was circumstantial; surely, you can criticize the opinion of a white person without hating white people or criticize the opinion of a black person without hating black people.

But unfortunately, in today's dialogue, immutable traits—the things about us that we cannot control—are used against people oftentimes even more so than the things they actually say. When you reason with immutable traits (e.g., their gender, ethnicity, resources, etc.) about an individual rather than the substance of their speech, you are past the point of empathy: you are at the point of assigning blame. To boot, nothing about my insistence of *nil nisi bonum de mortuis ("do not speak ill of the dead")* reeks of racism, and as you will see shortly, I extend that same philosophy to the late Kobe Bryant. When you say "you only feel that way because you are X" or "you only feel that way because you are Y," you are actually just telling someone (for them) the reason why they hold their beliefs rather than letting them tell you how they came to their own conclusions. It is really a backhanded way of telling a person that they lack empathy, because you are suggesting that they are unable to put themselves in your shoes due to a limiting factor outside of their control. The obvious reason why this is a faulty line of reasoning goes beyond the lack of empathy in such a position; no group of people—black, white, straight, gay, man, woman, etc.—is a monolith with a uniform set of ideas. So to suggest that someone's contrary viewpoint to your own can only be deduced by any of these immutable traits suggests the opposite: that all such people should act or think a certain way. And if George Orwell's *1984* was any indication, groupthink is not something we should aspire to.

Nowhere is the lack of empathy in our society today more prevalent than in the idea of "canceling" people and their entire careers for past transgressions. Mere minutes after Kobe Bryant's death in a freak helicopter accident was reported, overzealous reporters like Felicia Sonmez of the *Washington Post* and a handful of other opportunistic social media personalities were all too eager to remind people of the rape allegation against him from nearly two decades prior. I find such behavior abhorrent, as it seeks out the worst thing someone did, amplifies it, and implies that the person's death may be justified. How crass have we become that we celebrate death—as many did in the aftermath of the deaths of John McCain or Ruth Bader Ginsburg—and tarnish their name immediately?

Those who partake in cancel culture behave as if they have lived perfect lives. At least one would think so based on the way that mistakes are singled out—oftentimes from decades ago—and weaponized against an individual to destroy their career. Who among us has not said or done something that they later on regretted? It is true for almost everyone except maybe the Dalai Lama. If we treated the cancel people the same way they treat their victims, there would be no cancel people left to cancel others. In most cases, people are sincerely apologetic for the mistakes of their past. But this is no matter for the cancel people. Everything must be stripped away as penance. For what it's worth, I sometimes empathize with the people who are canceling others, because I imagine their intentions are good: they want the world to be a better place. And sometimes, it is good to speak up. For example, there are of course people like Harvey Weinstein who deserve to be cast away forever. However, what we are finding more and more is that this desire to purify our society is being applied to others over philosophical disagreement. I find that dangerous because the inevitable end of that road is the end of discourse, and at the end of discourse, the only option left is violence. Look no further than Ellen Degeneres, who was widely repudiated for hanging out with George W. Bush at a football game. Ironically, it was later on for accusations about the environment of her show's workplace that Ellen's career came under negative scrutiny—and perhaps appropriately so.

I encourage the reader to think long and hard about the legitimate reasons why someone else might have formed a different opinion—like their upbringing or their life experiences versus your own. Experiences like these have convinced me that, more than ever, it is important to understand how to apply the sales mindset—and empathy in particular—to our increasingly tense conversations. Because I have taken this empathetic attitude with others, I have found myself able to have reasonable dialogue with many people of varying political stripes. Over the last few years, I have fostered conversations with people on both the left and right sides of the political spectrum. As someone who is in the political center, I am often frustrated by friends on both sides—as they are with me. I do not profess to be perfect, and sometimes I wish I might have handled things better. But I have had a plethora of friends reach out to me from out of the blue to tell me one of two things. Some of them thank me for being a voice of reason, regardless of whether or not what I have to say is popular. Others thank me for providing the only space in their social sphere where reasonable, intelligent dialogue can occur between people of varying belief systems. That happens because I try to have a non-attachment to my own ideas as much as I possibly can. In other words, I accept the possibility that I might be wrong. We believe in the ideas we have—that is what makes them our ideas. What makes our ideas dangerous is having so much conviction in them that we do not welcome any sort of dialogue. In the absence of dialogue, your only option is violence. This is why I am intensely critical of both right-wing violence from anti-Semites, Islamophobes, and White nationalists just as much as I am of far left violence from members of antifa, and I generally have a hard time finding the patience for those who try to condone violence simply because of its source. In a way, they are playing with a different set of rules than I am—one where it is OK to lack empathy if the politics of the offender are similar to their own.

How then can we be more empathetic? Like most desirable attributes, it is a lot easier said than done.

First and foremost, untie your reaction, your assumption, your emotion, and so on, from how you are going to respond. In fact, you might need to untie the individual from your response if you have a specific history with that individual.

Ask yourself what are the alternatives that can be true, and what is the likelihood of each alternative. Most importantly, ask questions and seek to understand. There is an instinct when we are upset about something to tell the other person why they are wrong. Asking questions helps you to uncover what someone is really saying. It might confirm your original hypothesis, but you might be surprised and uncover new information that makes the conversation much easier to have.

Recently, I sat down with a prospective customer to walk through a return on investment. We had already prepared a return on investment analysis and the customer had agreed about the numbers. My instinct when I was told that they wanted to do this exercise once more was that this must be a way to try to goad us into offering better pricing. In my mind, I had decided that they might skew some of the numbers to try to convince me to offer a lower price.

However, I approached that conversation with genuine interest in understanding the math. They had truly done their research and came very prepared with even minutiae of detail we had not yet considered. In the end, they did indeed present to me a different picture of the return on investment. However, I had noticed a major mistake along the way and I pointed it out to them. They agreed about the mistake, we adjusted the numbers to be more or less similar to what they were originally, and we all moved on. Had I come into that conversation ready to point fingers, asking angrily why we even needed to do this exercise again, I probably would have created a bad feeling in the customer's mind. In fact, I would venture to say they would no longer be interested in working with me.

2020 was a very tense year. I have seen too many of my friends completely write off the people who disagree with them. Remember, no one is trying to suck on purpose. No one wakes up every day with a picture of you on their wall thinking about how they are going to mess up your day. From an evolutionary perspective, human beings are doing whatever they can to protect themselves and to do the best they can. There are unique circumstances behind the way each and every one of us think. Try to remember that next time you want to punch someone in the face.

Part II

Looking back on some of my own experiences, there is one time in my life that is particularly profound to me when thinking about empathy. Your college years are supposed to be the best years of your life, but for me some of that time was incredibly dark and sad. I remember how excited I was for the opportunity to go to Princeton. It was my dream school so I applied there early decision. I awaited the day that I would receive their decision in the mail, and to this day, I can still remember every detail of walking to the mailbox, feeling excited that it was a big envelope, reading about my acceptance during the short walk to the house, and hugging my mother who was probably ten times more excited than I was.

Getting into college was a huge weight off my shoulders. I went to a very regimented and competitive all-boys' high school where about 20% of my peers all received early entry into Harvard. On top of the stress of competing with these ultra-talented peers, I also lived in the shadow of an over-achieving older brother who traveled the world winning debate tournaments, who got straight A's, and who eventually was admitted to Yale. I was happy to be done with the stress for a while and to turn the chapter—and go to school with girls.

In high school, I was my authentic self, and for that, I was rewarded. I was voted Varsity Wrestling Captain and I held leadership positions in many clubs and organizations. I was not necessarily the most popular person in my class, but I had good relationships with most people, and to this day, I still make a habit of staying in touch with many of my classmates. Even though I was not in the top 10% of my class, I received one of four major awards handed out to my class and to this day I consider that to be one of my proudest achievements.

In college, things took a very sharp turn for me. My senior year of high school had been difficult for me in many ways, particularly with the death of a close friend in a car crash and the subsequent survivor's guilt I felt a month later when I had my own near-death car crash. People I had trusted let me down. I was depressed, and that angst carried its way into college, where I tried desperately to regain my footing by being liked by other people. Losing sight of who I was ended up being my greatest mistake.

My desire to fit in had me acting in ways that were not truly reflective of who I was, and it turned some people off. Princeton has social hierarchies in the form of "Eating Clubs," which are really like co-ed fraternities and sororities where members also meet to eat meals three times a day and host parties on nights and weekends. These social strata were often dictated by groups you were affiliated with—sports teams, Greek life, a capella groups, etc.

Without getting into too much detail, I was unsuccessful in getting into the club of my choice where all of my friends hung out. This was, unfortunately, a social death knell for me. I was so upset when I found out about it that I left the campus and did not return until classes resumed the following week. I was embarrassed to see anyone, especially when I found out what some of these people had been saying about me behind closed doors.

So, when my friends would be eating their meals together, I was eating alone in my dorm room. Every so often there would be members-only parties at these clubs to which I was not invited. I truly felt like an outsider. I would often cry and lament about some of the decisions I had made. I did not understand what had happened to the old, authentic me that people used to admire. For the first time in my life, I felt like an absolute failure.

There were probably two things that helped me to hold everything together. One—and most importantly—was my best friend and eventual college roommate, Jeff. Jeff was in my fraternity, was a Varsity Volleyball captain, and he was a member of the club I wanted to be part of. Despite that, he felt exactly the way that I felt—like he did not belong. Jeff is the nicest person I have ever known and being a little socially awkward made him feel like he was an outsider, too. Like me, he felt that we were surrounded by a somewhat phony social system, and that we were not exactly being true to ourselves by participating in it. Ironically, he could see who I really was, and in my moment of greatest need, he reached out to me to start hanging out, for no other reason really than that he knew I needed it and that he knew we secretly had more in common than I would have realized.

The second thing that helped me hold things together emotionally were my studies. I had been rejected by the Creative Writing program when I first applied to college, but after honing my work a bit, I was accepted later during my freshman year and retained my spot by applying every semester thereafter. I enjoyed that immensely. The people in my classes were a very different mixture of people than the ones who I normally interacted with socially, and in that world, I felt like I had a fresh start, being able to write about whatever was on my mind and just getting things off my chest.

Eventually, in the spring of my senior year, I joined one of the eating clubs that anyone was allowed to join. For three and a half years, I had convinced myself that I was "too cool" for that. It turned out I was wrong. I remember being so angry with myself for having written people off without knowing them. That semester was the best semester I had—and it was the last one I had. I finally felt like I belonged somewhere, and people were very kind to me. But it was fleeting.

Throughout my college experience and for several years after I left, I resented everything about Princeton. I blamed everything about what had happened on other people. I told myself that it was a cutthroat place with narcissistic maniacs who were interested in stepping on the backs of other people if it helped them to climb the social ladder. When I received phone calls about donating to the school, I would lecture whoever was calling me about how elitist Princeton was and how I would never make a donation. To say I was bitter would be an understatement. Even by my fifth-year reunion, I remember both Jeff and I being sad to be back because we felt like we did not belong to any of the cliques that had been formed.

Something changed though in the last few years.

First and foremost, I recognized the flaws in who I was. I am a very different person today than I was a decade ago. I am a lot more thoughtful, a lot more curious, a lot more open-minded about people, and much kinder. I am far from perfect, but I am a better person today than I was back then, and I stopped being ashamed of admitting that. It was only by recognizing the flaws in myself and forgiving myself that I was able to start forgiving other people.

In light of what I now understood about myself—that I was a young guy just trying to navigate a complex social circle and fit in—did it not make sense that others around me were doing the exact same thing? Was it possible that others had made some immature decisions that they also regretted? Was it possible—if not likely—that some of the people who had spent years trying to exclude me had decided with the same benefit of hindsight that they had wronged me and wished that they had acted differently? And the most painful recognition of all—wasn't there at least some reason why I might have given some people a reason to turn their back on me? After all, we only got snippets of one another. It is very difficult to know someone entirely, let alone well.

Once I had asked myself these difficult questions, my attitudes started to change. When I would run into the people who had created this traumatic experience for me, I killed them with kindness instead of running away. I started to get more involved with the alumni community and to engage more with my classmates.

If anything, I made a habit of trying to engage more with a lot of the people whom I had scoffed at back when I was in college. But my engagement has been personally rewarding in many ways. I have traveled to Iowa City and Stillwater, OK to watch the wrestling team with other wrestling alumni and have attended every NCAA Wrestling Tournament over the last five years with the same group of people. I go back to reunions annually and I consider it the best three days of the year. I regularly talk about all sorts of things with a diverse group of alumni online, and though we do not always agree on things, I find myself learning instead of writing people off like I used to do. In fact, something I have realized through my social media interactions is that there were a lot more people in college who had had very positive opinions about me than I had remembered. And that is because I had spent so much of my time focusing on what I did not have versus what I did have. I had literally overlooked the existence of these people who I had gotten along with swimmingly simply because they did not belong to the social organization I wanted to belong to, and that in some ways is a reflection of my past lack of empathy. I was actually recently elected as the Vice President of my class, and I view my desire to take on that role as a testament to the progress I have made working on myself.

In order for my attitudes to change over time, I needed to do three things.

First, I needed to recognize that I was flawed. I think it is impossible to exhibit empathy towards other people if someone considers themself to be perfect. If you consider yourself to be perfect, you assume that everything you do is right, and therefore anyone who criticizes you must be wrong. Only when you allow for the possibility that you might be wrong can you start to see that everyone can be flawed, and you can start to relate to what you see as the flaws in other people since you recognize those flaws in yourself. One way to recognize your flaws is to detach yourself somewhat from your own ideas. At the end of the day, our ideas are formed as a combination of our backgrounds and upbringing (e.g., our predisposition to think in a certain way), as well as whatever information we have on hand. Both of those variables are exactly that: variables. That means they can change. And when you change variables, you change outcomes. If you had a different upbringing and a different set of facts to work off of, you could reasonably get to entirely different conclusions. So how are you to know if your set of circumstances in life makes you right? It is only through letting go and not needing to be right about everything that you can see yourself being wrong, and understand others being right. Of course, there are issues we are all deeply passionate about for which it is unlikely that our minds might be changed. Regardless, if you have dialogue with others under the assumption that you are right, you will end up positioning your opinions as facts, leaving out possibilities to find middle ground.

The second thing I needed to do was to forgive myself. I knew I could have gone about things in a better way back in college, but I still blamed other people because doing that was a lot easier than blaming myself. To be sure, some of the ideas I had about Princeton do ring true. But I needed to hold myself accountable and also forgive myself for any mistakes I had made. My heart was truly in the right place: I wanted to have friends. I was young and I learned a lesson. It did not need to dictate everything about who

I was. Once I had established some confidence in who I truly was as a person, I was able to forgive the younger me who had made mistakes but who I knew had also really tried his best adapting to a very different environment. This is very important. If you choose to look at yourself through a dark lens, you will have a hard time looking at others in a positive light. Bitterness and resentment are formed towards others when we adopt self-deprecating mindsets. When you start to see yourself as a good, well-intentioned person in all the things that you do—even when you make mistakes— you start to accept the possibility that other people might also be good, well-intentioned people behind the veil as well, even when their actions infuriate you.

Last but not least, I needed to forgive others. And as I said before, you cannot forgive and empathize with others until you forgive and empathize with yourself. Seeing my own flaws made me aware that we all have flaws. Seeing that I was just trying my best made me realize that most of us are also trying our best, even if we piss people off in the process. Telling myself that this was a version of me from a long time ago made me remember that this was also an everyone else of a long time ago, too. And I also realized that, all along, I had discounted many people who were my friends in college and who had always been kind to me, but that I was too preoccupied with my own apparent suffering to properly notice.

Today, I am really proud to call myself a Princeton alumnus. While I certainly regret momentarily losing grasp of my authentic self, it's not worth it any more to dwell on it. If I wish I could have done anything differently, I wish I had branched out more and spent more time with people who made me feel more confident in being me. I wish I had taken advantage of all the resources there—the speakers who were brought to campus, the various groups I could have joined, and so on. In sum, I have used the experience to vow to be me and to make sure I get the most out of my own curiosity rather than just doing what I think will make everyone else happy.

As I am writing this, racial tensions in our country are at an all-time high. There are issues with people who are overtly racists, and these people clearly lack empathy. But then there are also people who call people racists simply for having differing policy positions. I always find it fascinating that those people believe that that is a winning strategy in discourse, to call other people names. Ironically, these name-callers—who are basically asserting that others lack empathy—also lack empathy. They have eliminated all possibilities about the motives of the other person except the possibility that fits their own worldview, which is that one must be a racist to disagree with them. When you call someone a name (any name at all), you are past the point of seeking to understand. Almost always, it probably means you have not practiced the exercises of Cognitive-Behavioral Therapy, which would ask you to consider all alternative possibilities to name-calling. When you call someone a name, you do so knowing full well that the other person will not change their behavior. This means that the name-calling is done out of self-interest in being right about something, and not for the sake of helping the other person.

There is a very simple rule you can follow here: if you have hard evidence to substantiate an opinion, use it. If you only have circumstantial evidence, do not use it. Unless someone has declared that they are a certain "thing," chances are you only have circumstantial evidence that they are, indeed, that "thing."

Here is an example of that. Let's say you get stood up for a meeting. That would give you some circumstantial evidence that the other person does not respect your time. Yet, it would be a terrible idea to tell that person the next time you hear from them that they do not respect your time. You have no idea if they had a medical emergency, a family emergency, or just a simple misunderstanding. All you have is circumstantial evidence to support a conclusion you have drawn. What would be hard evidence is if the person actually acknowledged that they stood you up intentionally. I had this happen to me many years ago when I flew to another city for a meeting and the person I was supposed to meet with was not there. When I called him to ask where he was, he told me he forgot to cancel our meeting and was somewhere else that day. Fortunately, I had other meetings to go to in that city, and I kept my calm.

At its core, empathy is about understanding how people got from Point A to Point B. We assume too much about other peoples' intentions. Information provides great power. The more information we have, the greater our capability to be empathetic. In the absence of information, all we have are snap judgments with a greater variability in their accuracy. Empathy is acknowledging to yourself that you, too, have flaws, and that it is only by getting more information that you can truly form an opinion.

We were all innocent children once. We all are formed by different circumstances and experiences, many of which are out of our control. Not to get too existential, but we really have very little understanding of why we are here, what is our own consciousness, or what our role is in a very large universe. We are but specks of dust in the grand scheme of things trying to do our best to get by. From this perspective, it becomes a lot easier to view people as just like us, no matter how reprehensible their opinions might be. In our attempts to figure out how to get by in this world, we have all done things that we regret. And while I am not suggesting that you need to just accept being wronged whenever you are, it is important to at least acknowledge the flaws of our human nature before rushing to judgment.

Next time you find yourself judging another person for doing something you disagree with, remind yourself of your own flaws. Do you want to be the type of person who does not acknowledge that they are flawed? Once you come to terms with your own problems (and let's face it, we all have many problems, no matter what type of image we portray on social media), you start to see other people as no different than yourself. And it is only when you start to relate to people in this way that you can begin to start planting new ideas in their mind: Inception.

Chapter 4

Inception

In the 2010 film *Inception*, Leonardo DiCaprio's character, Dom Cobb, is responsible for a plot to plant an idea in the mind of another man, Robert Fisher. Cobb is employed by a man named Saito, and Saito wants Cobb to convince Robert to dissolve his company. Why? Because Robert's company is a direct competitor to Saito's company.

You might expect in a traditional environment that Saito would just approach Robert directly and negotiate with him about dissolving his company. This would certainly be the more direct approach. Saito would lay out his rationale for why this is a good idea and hope that the message is well-received.

But there is a big problem with that approach. When you tell someone to adopt your idea, it is your idea, not theirs. And people generally like ideas more when they are their own ideas. Saito—knowing he is a direct competitor to Robert—also realizes that there will be immediate mistrust between the two if he were to try to hatch his plan through direct discourse.

Something I see all too often today is people making other people feel stupid for *not* having the same idea. Think about any time you have ever logged on to Facebook and witnessed some sort of political argument between two people. How often is name-calling or sarcasm invoked as a means of making someone else feel stupid?

Making other people feel stupid—even if you are right—is almost never a winning strategy. Even if people ultimately end up agreeing with you, they will resent you for making them feel dumb and they will react stubbornly instead. If you were on a sales call with a prospect, you would hopefully never say something like, "How can you not see how good my product is for you?" Instead, you might be better served asking "How does my product make you feel?" since this is what you would probably organically ask any of your close friends or family when you are selling them on an idea and soliciting feedback.

So, what does Saito ultimately decide to do?

He asks Cobb to plant his idea passively into Robert's mind via a process known as "Inception." Inception is a process where you go into someone's subconscious via their dreams and essentially get the individual onboard with your idea by allowing a situation to unfold inside of their mind as they sleep. In this way, the individual whose dreams are under attack feels when they wake up that whatever it is you have planted in their mind was their idea all along—it is just something that came to them as they were dreaming.

In the movie, there are layers to the process of inception. For example, once you enter the dreams of your target subject, you can then enter the subject's dreams within the dream. And then you can continuously go deeper and deeper. The deeper you go, the more dangerous it gets. However, the deeper you go, the further you go into the subconscious to plant the idea, thereby making the idea even stronger.

Note how indirect this entire process is. Again, Saito has an opportunity to approach his target directly to negotiate with him, but he chooses not to. Instead, he hires a band of thieves to go into the dreams of his target, several layers into his subconscious. They are not even very direct with the idea that they plant in his head. They do not get several layers deep into Robert's subconscious and start yelling "Dissolve your company!" Instead, they get several layers deep and allow for Robert to have a moment with his dying father.

Throughout the film, you come to understand that Robert had tension with his recently deceased father. Robert had felt that his father was never proud of him and did not trust him to run the family business. Saito and his band of thieves look to exploit this personal dilemma. When they allow for Robert to have this moment with his father deep in his own subconscious, Robert's father tells him that he wants Robert to be his own man. Thus, when Robert wakes up, he has the resolve to dissolve his company, thinking now that this is what his father would have wanted him to do. In fact, the only reason he had not thought to dissolve his company sooner is because he had always felt that his father resented him for being an under-achiever. With that understanding, his resolve before inception was to run the company so successfully in order to prove his dead father wrong.

What makes this moment work so well for Saito is that Robert feels that he has come up with this idea to dissolve his company all by himself. He has no idea that the people around him have literally infiltrated his brain to plant the idea there. And this is exactly why it works so well: the idea is his own, not something that someone else foisted upon him—or at least not to his knowledge.

Inception happens organically in everyday life when you are naturally curious about people with whom you interact. We talked already about Cognitive Behavioral Therapy (CBT), for example, where patients are often asked to reason with scenarios that are possible that they might not have considered. CBT is relevant here because so much of good inception comes from simply asking people questions and getting them to talk themselves into the answers. A lot of times, people have simply not put themselves through the exercise of actually talking through something that is causing them anxiety. For example, let's say you are turned down in a job interview, and you never receive any feedback from your interviewer. Your immediate reaction might be to assume that they made a mistake. You might also decide that this company is incredibly rude to have taken up your time and then washed their hands of you without explanation. However, when you ask yourself what other possibilities might exist, it could be that you are over-qualified for the position. The company might be in turmoil and its employees too helter-skelter to prioritize you. Perhaps they just got too busy and it slipped their mind to follow up with you properly. These are all reasonable expectations with varying degrees of probability. But CBT might help you become aware of things organically that you had not previously considered. Perhaps in the course of recalling the chain of events, you are now able to recall that your interviewer did seem awfully stressed out and unfocused for much of time. Perhaps that is a cue that some of these alternative possibilities might be true.

I had a coworker who was very good at this idea of inception. He would introduce an idea and then get people to accept the idea through a series of questions. The way I explain this process to my sales team is as if you are a Sherpa taking your clients to the top of Mount Everest. You are not there to push them up the mountain; you are merely there to show them the way. They will do the climbing and the heavy lifting on their own. My co-worker was very good at inception because he asked open-ended questions that established a pain point that people would ultimately come to realize on their own, simply through being forced to answer questions they had not asked themselves previously.

However, my co-worker made one flaw when it came to his inception: he made it no secret that he was engaging in the craft. To be fair, he was good at it. But bragging about planting ideas in peoples' minds serves to do one thing: it makes them hyper-aware that you might be trying to do exactly that. This meant that as people started to converse with him more and more, they would start conversations by saying something like, "Don't you try your inception stuff on me." In other words, people were on their toes and calculating what kind of mind games might be imposed on them. What this implied to me is that although he was well-intended every time he engaged in inception, he generally had some sort of agenda whenever he was engaging in his special brand of inception. And while you certainly can be successful in sales by trying to engage in inception with an agenda, it becomes a lot more challenging once everyone knows what you are doing. This is why authentic, good-faith inception is something you should seek to achieve organically.

So, how do you organically plant ideas in peoples' minds? It sounds pretty challenging. But it's actually very easy, and we covered it in Chapter 2. You treat them the same way you treat your best friend.

Let's cover some examples so we can bring this to life.

Let's say my friend Brendan and I are trying to make plans this evening. We have both voiced an interest in seeing the same new movie that has come out. I have decided that this would be a great option for us for the evening, so I propose that we go see it. Brendan replies that he is interested in seeing the movie, but he is really hungry and he has been wanting to try a new restaurant around the corner.

The way many people might respond in this situation is by foisting the movie down Brendan's throat. That might consist of a few different tactics. One might be by suggesting that the movie has food and snacks which can satiate Brendan's hunger. Another tactic might be to find a way to do both—perhaps by first eating at the restaurant and then going to see the movie, or vice-versa. Or, you might just be downright dismissive, suggesting that the restaurant does not really have great reviews but that the movie has been critically acclaimed. And to be sure, you might be successful in getting your way in any of the aforementioned scenarios, it just does not make you a very good friend. What also happens when you try any of these approaches is that Brendan certainly knows that your plan is at odds with his. You are no longer having a conversation and you are now instead having something of a pseudo-argument about whose idea is best.

Being a good friend would actually be quite simple. Being a good friend would be to ask Brendan why he is so interested in the restaurant. This question puts your ego aside and removes your own assumptions and biases (e.g., the premonition that the movie is the best plan), and allows your curiosity to take hold. And if you are a good friend, you will mean it when you ask that question, because you will be equally invested in an outcome that suits Brendan as you would be in an outcome that suits yourself. And it is entirely possible that Brendan's description of the restaurant will change your mind. Since you have so many things in common, it is likely that you will end up acknowledging that the restaurant does indeed seem pretty awesome, which at bare minimum serves to validate Brendan's own feelings. Once you have a mutual understanding of aligned interests and goals, the conversation no longer feels antagonistic. On your own, you are likely both to come to the conclusion that the restaurant is brand new, it will be around for a while, but the movie will only be in theaters for a matter of weeks. And with that, you might naturally come to the conclusion that the movie should be the focal point of the evening—but you are willing to accommodate the restaurant or some other food beforehand if you can make it work with the movie times.

Of course, being a good friend runs the proverbial risk that you may not get what you originally set out to gain. That is OK. We all too often consider ourselves winners or losers based on what our original goals were. This is a terrible mistake, because we assume that the goals we set for ourselves are ironclad. It leaves out the possibility that we are missing new information that might change the way we think and feel about the world around us. Brendan's description of the restaurant might be so amazing that you realize you can just go see the movie the next day with someone else, lest you pass up an opportunity to try this new place.

In a traditional sales setting, this means you need to be ready to steer your customer to a solution that is not yours. This is considered "losing" in the sales world, but that has certainly not been my experience. Something I have been particularly proud of in my career is the bevy of customers who have said "no" to me countless times who eventually said "yes." Every single time this has happened, they told me the same thing: "It took me awhile to get to you, but I always looked at you as someone who was being authentic, telling the truth, and genuinely trying to help me. So I trust that you are not going to let me down." I am not making this up for the sake of driving a narrative home in my book; some of my best customers have said "no" to me and eventually said "yes," citing the authenticity in my approach as a leading factor in their decision.

There have been times when I have invited prospects to client entertainment events and nice dinners and they have said things like, "I feel bad accepting your invitation because we already use your competitor's technology and I don't want you to waste a spot on me that you could be using on someone who is ready to buy right now." I always laugh at this and insist that they come. If your sole intention in having these events is to sell someone a product, the entire vibe and atmosphere of the event will feel as such and it will probably be less successful than you think, no matter how much everyone drinks or how much they laugh. People do not want to be made to feel like you can just buy their business. They want to be made to feel like you are invested in their success, and that includes taking them at their best (as your customer) and at their worst (when they work with your competitor).

I try instead to fill the room with people that I like hanging out with and who I know my customers and prospects will enjoy being around. I prioritize my paying customers first before my potential prospects and beyond that, I try not to have any agenda. My goal is to create a forum for people to network and share best practices with one another. My personal goal is to build relationships with people so that I can start to care about their interests the way I care about my friends. If I do that well, then the time will come down the road where the people in that room will feel the same way about me because we are, indeed, friends. And what stems from that is an opportunity at some time and place to get my hat in the ring to sell my product, which I genuinely feel is beneficial to that customer. If, on the other hand,

I turn the people away who are not ready to buy my product, they will remember that they were only invited for a specific, agenda-driven reason. Certainly not to become their friend. If and when an opportunity arises in the future, I will probably not be high on the list of people to call.

A situation like this actually recently just happened in my sales career. A couple years ago, I had reached out to a prospect at a major life insurance company. I knew they were using the technology of one of our competitors, so I positioned the conversation as a high-level introduction. This individual told me that he had actually recently left his company and that he did not want to waste my time with a conversation. Instead of agreeing with him (since he purportedly had no immediate value to me, in his eyes), I suggested we still network with one another because you never know what we might learn from one another or if we could help each other out someday. We ended up staying in touch periodically, and I referred him to several consulting roles from within my professional network, which helped him out financially and professionally as he figured out what he wanted to do. I never had any expectation that someday he might try to return the favor because I helped with a sincere interest in helping out. I just found out via LinkedIn that he has landed with one of the largest online retailers in the planet, and as I am writing this, he just reached out to me with hopes of finally connecting about the product that I sell.

Inception occurs naturally when you do not have an agenda. When there is no agenda, you end up showing rather than telling. There is a difference, for example, between a leader who yells at everyone on his team, ordering them to do various tasks, and a leader who just does those tasks himself. When the team sees the leader doing the tasks, they are motivated to do those tasks as well. This is called "leading by example."

Here is a good real-world example of that. There is a black man named Daryl Davis who has spent much of his time over the last 30 years converting more than 200 Ku Klux Klan members to leave and denounce the KKK. Yes, you read that right. I was amazed when I heard about this story myself. I cannot imagine the amount of empathy one must have to take on such a task, but Mr. Davis clearly harbors enough of it to see past the most vitriolic hatred our country has ever seen. His tactic for convincing these people to change their ideas did not come through a series of lectures. He did not get 200 people into a room and give them a presentation on racism. Instead, he befriended them. What happened was that the people he befriended started to realize for themselves that Mr. Davis was just a fantastic human being. They came to regret their past decisions and to feel a sense of shame on their own accord. Mr. Davis taught them just by being who he was that you should not hold prejudices based on the color of someone's skin. My intention here is not to advocate for anyone to tolerate racism or bigotry in any of its forms; in fact, I have no tolerance for it myself as someone who has sometimes been the victim of anti-Semitic rhetoric. Instead, it is simply to show how powerful Inception can be. Even in the most extreme circumstances, Inception can be a powerful tool.

It is usually more powerful to feel the force of an idea through osmosis rather than by having someone tell it to you. Think about any good story or movie you have ever seen. Chances are, there was a theme accompanying the story or the film, one that probably resonated with you much more than any sort of sentence or statement of fact possibly could. Think about the notion of racism in the United States. We all have our own ideas about the prevalence of racism that we gathered from history books growing up, talking to other people, watching the news, and what have you. That said, Jordan Peele's movies *Get Out* and *Us* are both so eloquent in their commentary on racism in the United States that even those who might have felt they already had a firm understanding on the role of racism in our society are forced to reconcile with the ideas of the films. Why is that?

Well, generally speaking, people like to figure things out for themselves. In his book *The Subtle Art of Not Giving a F*ck,* author Mark Manson gives an example about a person running a marathon. In it, he lays out two scenarios: one where you have a gun to your head to run a marathon (or die), and another where you decide to do it for yourself and accomplish it. In both scenarios, the act of running the marathon is indeed unpleasant for the average person. But at least in the latter scenario there is a feeling of accomplishment and achievement. That is because when you decide to do something for yourself and you do it, you feel a lot better than doing that same thing when it is ordered by someone else. If you spent your entire day doing chores, for example, you might feel by the end of the day that you had a productive day. But if you did those chores because your parent or significant other ordered you to do them, you would probably feel that you missed out on having a productive day, because you were never actually doing what you wanted to be doing.

The same is true for inception. This is why telling a customer that your product is great does not mean very much. For one thing, it is your idea—not theirs. Also, statements are not always reality, and most people know that. This is also why most dialogue falls flat between people who disagree about serious issues today. For example, when someone is called a name (e.g., "racist," "idiot," or "snowflake") at the beginning of a conversation, odds are that they will tune out. However, if you showed that same person some compelling, non-negotiable data, then you are now creating a possibility for someone to see your side through osmosis—through being shown—rather than being told. The approach of name-calling as if this will somehow turn them into a better person is misguided because people want to come to their conclusions on their own and not be told what their conclusions ought to be. By the way, anyone who is truly interested in generating a positive outcome for the world instead of "being right" and belittling another human being would naturally try to show versus tell. Show-ers are do-ers. Tellers are narcissists.

I learned about racism, for example, both explicitly and implicitly. I learned about it explicitly through what I was taught in school and what my parents taught me (e.g., to treat everyone with respect regardless of their skin color). But implicitly, I learned about it in high school. The high school I attended was racially and socioeconomically diverse, certainly more so than the public high school in the town where I grew up. And I found through that experience that everyone I knew had their own successes and flaws. I viewed my classmates as individuals, rather than as representatives of racial or ethnic or religious or socioeconomic groups, as that is how I wanted people to view me. That was not someone telling me what to feel, it was just me experiencing it for myself. For this reason, some of my closest friends then (and to this day) were those I had very little in common with on the surface.

But another way I learned about racism was implicitly. That happened when I was pulled over for speeding not long ago with my close friend, who is a Black man, in the passenger seat. I watched him put his hands up in the air so the officer could see them the whole time. He later told me how scared he was during the entire interaction once it was over. I, too, was nervous interacting with the officer but it definitely never crossed my mind that he might shoot me. That experience taught me more about the reality of racism, as it is lived by people of color, more than any other piece of information I could have been given. My takeaway here is simple: oftentimes it is the things unsaid that can go much further with people, because then they come to the ideas on their own without otherwise being told by you what to think.

When you use Inception, you move from telling people how to feel and you allow them to see it for themselves. The authors of these books and the directors of these movies could very simply grab a megaphone and tell you the message they want you to accept. They don't do that. They showcase the story instead because it allows you as the reader or the viewer to reach their conclusion on your own. You are able to reach your conclusion on your own because you do not even realize you are being sold on the message. That is what makes it feel authentic to you. I am a big M. Night Shyamalan fan, but his film *The Happening* received some of the worst reviews a movie has ever received because its message about environmental conservation is so over the top— that humanity must die in order for the planet to live—that you question whether he is being serious. To be sure, environmental conservation is a concept most people support. But if the message is so extreme and hackneyed that the viewer becomes aware from the get-go that they are being sold the cinematic equivalent of a defective product, chances are that they will not adopt the idea as their own. They may even adopt contrary ideas. Ironically then, it is through subtlety—implicit understanding—that you achieve Inception. In the world of selling, this means you need to find ways for your points to be made on their own, and for that to happen, the customer needs to be doing most of the talking—not you.

In his book *Positive Intelligence,* author Shirzad Chamine talks about saboteurs we all have in our brains and how we can use various mindfulness tactics to activate what he calls "the PQ brain." The PQ brain recognizes the saboteurs as mere noise and uses them in a positive way. Chamine argues that fear-based selling does not activate the PQ brain. Fear-based selling is when you essentially try to scare someone into doing something. Liken it to when you were a child and you were told that a monster living in your closet might come out and scare you if you did not eat your vegetables or do all your homework. I agree with Chamine, in large part because fear-based selling is largely not the way we interact with the people we care about. It is not to say that we cannot make recommendations to people that are not predicated on fear of the alternative; it is instead to say that there must be some sincerity when we do it.

If my best friend was drunk and insisted on driving somewhere to do something that they felt was an urgent need, of course I would never let them get in a car. My rationale, by default, would be fear-based: "you are going to get yourself and maybe someone else killed, and you will get arrested." That rationale would be borne of necessity, because those are the obvious facts. And by giving that advice, I would be genuinely interested in the best outcome for my best friend. In a vacuum, what happens to my friend does not directly impact me, so my desire for their safety is predicated on their interests, and my fear-based 'selling' is simply based on reality.

What I would not do is use manipulative fear tactics. I would not resort to something like, "I will never talk to you again," or "your family would disown you." Because I would not know if either of those two things are true. It is certainly possible I would be disappointed enough in my friend that they would ignore simple advice, or that their family might be enraged with them for getting a DUI. But those fears are speculative and borne of my imagination in an attempt to get what I want. And generally those are the types of things that might come out of my mouth if my interest is self-interest—that I do not want to be held accountable for letting my drunk friend get in a car, or that I do not want to live with the guilt of doing so. We see stuff like this all the time in the sales world with looming deadlines for better pricing or sales reps suggesting to customers they hardly know what a cataclysmic outcome they will realize in the absence of the product that is being sold. If you do not like when salespeople do it to you, do not do it to other people.

Shirzad Chamine also talks about the paradox of having to let go of needing the sale in order to get the sale. Basically, he gives an example where someone asks him a simple question: "If I am authentic in my interactions with a customer, is it not possible that I might lead them to not buying from me, or worse, buying

from a competitor?" Chamine's counter-point is that merely having such a thought is allowing the saboteurs in your brain to have
a larger role than they should have. Such a fear is completely
speculative and is only allowed to spread if you do not see it for
what it is—a mere thought that stems from our fight-or-flight
reflex and our survival instincts. Instead, he would argue allowing
your real character to be on display will give you the best possible
chance to close the sale, because other people can sense when you
are radiating real, genuine positivity. And while I acknowledge
this is not going to be true 100% of the time (let's face it, no one
closes 100% of deals), I do agree with that as a general trend and
I have found that to be true in my own interactions. Specifically,
I have found this to be true when potential clients of mine end up
moving forward with another vendor. What they find in interacting with me is that my demeanor remains unchanged. I do not
become bitter or start to act like I never knew them. On the contrary, I continue trying to provide them with value, as if nothing
changed. Once a representative from one of the country's largest
healthcare companies told me explicitly that they were electing to
work with me precisely because of the way I had behaved when
they chose to work instead with our competitor, which ultimately
did not work out for them. If we all could eliminate our need for
immediate gratification (which I know is easier said than done),
we would end up being able to build much better and longer-term
relationships than the ones we get by being disingenuous, which
usually leads to needing to apologize for something later down
the road.

Inception is often accomplished through authentic story-telling and being vulnerable. I have already described how it is better

to show than tell, and story-telling (despite its name) is really a great way of making a point. A lot of the stories that I tell to my customers are things that I have seen work and not work for other clients, whether it is with my product or another strategy altogether. In this way, I remove myself as the salesperson and turn myself into more of an objective consultant. My client feels they are getting a fair representation of how everything works because I am indeed giving them a fair representation, and not only does this help build trust that I will be honest with them, it also shows them that I know what I am talking about. In this way, the customer is able to realize the value of my product for themself, without me needing to spell it out clearly.

Thinking broadly about applying this principle in everyday life, I would encourage my reader to think about being vulnerable with other people. The times I have garnered the most respect from members of my team or even amongst my friends, I think, are when I acknowledge some shortcoming of mine and how I am working to overcome it. Yes, we all idolize celebrities and athletes for all of the great things they do and we respect them for all of their hard work. But we have a tendency to respect even more those who made mistakes and atoned for them, or who fell short in some regard and then made a miraculous comeback. And that is precisely because overcoming adversity is attractive to us as human beings. We are biologically wired to want to overcome adversity for our own survival, and we find it admirable when others are able to do so. It takes a big person to admit their own flaws. When I sit down with the people I manage, I make a point of calling out times in my past where I have made mistakes. Indeed, you will see me calling out my own mistakes throughout this book. I don't do any of this because I want people to respect me. That would not be authentic. I do it because the stories are all true, I learned from those stories, and I think others can learn from them too. And my job as a manager is to make the people who work for me stronger. If that entails embarrassing myself from time to time to cast light on my past mistakes, then so be it. If there is anything I know to be true, it is that they will respect me far more for acknowledging my humanity than if I just told them all the great things I do every day and why they should follow my lead. So when you deal with other people in everyday life and negotiate for yourself, be more willing—not less willing—to shed light on your own flaws. You will get much further that way than you will when you dig your heels in and pretend that you are perfect all of the time. Especially in tense and difficult conversations, like around politics or family-related matters, be willing to show how your ideas have evolved and why your ideas of yesterday were flawed. It will naturally (and usually subconsciously) signal to the other individual that you are reasonable.

There is a real-world example of this that I will gladly share, and it has to do with mental health. There has been a movement lately to de-stigmatize mental health issues, and I think that is a good thing. But it still feels taboo for some people. I wrote a blog not long ago that talked about my own journey with mental health challenges. Specifically, it was about sudden, unexplainable panic attacks I was starting to randomly have in face-to-face meetings with customers. Because I had had a couple of these panic attacks in those settings, I had psyched myself into having them during other minutiae of my life, like while getting a haircut. Now, writing that blog was risky in some ways because a future employer could read it and think that maybe I have some issues they do not want to take on. Alternatively, a future employer who might refuse to hire me for writing a blog designed to help others and make them feel safer in their own skin might not be the type of employer I want to work for. My point here is that being vulnerable feels to a lot of people like it only has downside, but in reality, I think it only has upside. When you are vulnerable, you weed out the people who cannot handle it, and you instead embrace the people who appreciate you for having taken a risk that most people would not have the authenticity to tackle head on.

Another real-world example of how vulnerability shines is in comedy. When your friends make a joke about their own ineptitude, you may be more apt to find it funny since there is sincerity behind the joke. In fact, many famous comedians are known for their self-deprecating humor. Comics often speak of their lives as dark, lonely, and depressing, and yet people still find a way to laugh. This is probably because the audience finds the storylines to be realistic.

I want to come full circle and get back to asking questions. You generally find yourself more willing to ask questions sincerely of your close friends and family because you actually want the information you are looking for. Through a series of questions, your close friend or family member is likely to have some sort of epiphany on their own simply for being forced to answer questions they had not been asking themselves previously. This is why talk therapy is such a popular phenomenon that works for people to combat their anxieties. In talk therapy, patients often talk themselves into a solution simply by talking out their problems.

In cognitive-behavioral therapy, the therapist asks questions that force the patient to consider alternatives to the truth they have accepted for themselves. The key here is asking questions that you naturally feel compelled to ask. Most good salespeople are taught to ask questions as part of their selling philosophy. But just asking questions for the sake of asking questions is meaningless. When you are asking questions because your sales manager told you to—because it makes the customer seem like you are interested in what they have to say, or because it gives you information that purportedly allows you to tailor the conversation to them—you are really asking out of self-interest. You are not asking out of their interests. This is obviously problematic from an authenticity perspective.

My philosophy is simple: you are more likely to get from Point A to Point B by just caring about your customer the way you care about a close friend. If you are able to achieve this, you will find yourself naturally asking the questions that you should be asking. And you will be asking those questions because you want to ask those questions. Using a question to try to pigeon-hole a customer into giving you a certain response you want might feel rewarding in the moment, but deep down it is likely that the customer is registering the lack of passion behind what you are asking whether consciously or subconsciously. You will naturally "plant the idea" in your customer's head via Inception by caring, just as most close friends are able to help resolve each other's issues simply by caring, listening, and offering suggestions.

Chapter 5

Cold Outreach, or,
"Weirder Than Waldo"

Very few salespeople enjoy cold calling a new prospect. You are interrupting someone's day, they have no idea who you are, and most often, they figure out pretty quickly that you are trying to sell them something. Rejection is inevitable. And sometimes that rejection manifests itself in very cruel ways—prospects asking you to never call them again or to take you off their list.

I am conditioned to be wary of cold calls because I remember growing up that telemarketers would call our home multiple times a day trying to sell us something. My home phone would ring at least once a day with some new telemarketer trying to sell us something. God forbid the telemarketer called during dinner and got an earful from one of my parents. It was grilled into me at a pretty young age that these unsolicited phone calls were unwelcome.

The fear of cold calling is really not very different than any other fear of rejection we experience in our everyday lives. Many of the people who are nervous about making a cold call are often the same people who would be hesitant to try to befriend a random stranger. But rejection does not just manifest itself in the more overt or traditional settings we might think of, like the classic scenario of a guy trying to pick a girl up at the bar. We also fear rejection in the risks we decide not to take every day.

I will use my own story as an example. Writing has always been my passion. I was planning on majoring in Economics in college, but halfway through my sophomore year, I had a change of heart, realizing I was "selling my soul" a bit by pursuing a future on Wall Street. I had only really set my sights on Economics because I liked business and I thought I would make a lot of money doing it. But truth be told, I did not really enjoy it. I did enjoy reading and writing, so I decided to major in English and Creative Writing instead. This is obviously a very big change:

going from the objective science of Economics, which would all but guarantee me a high-paying job after college, to majoring in the very subjective art of English and Creative Writing, where my future job prospects would be much slimmer.

When it came time for me to find a job, I knew deep down what I *wanted* to do if I did not have to worry about money. That was to move to Los Angeles and become a screenwriter. But that is not what I ended up doing. What I ended up doing instead was taking a sales job. And the reason I took that sales job was because I wanted to make enough money so that I could create the financial freedom for myself to pursue what I actually wanted to pursue—writing. And over the decade that followed, I have had a very successful sales career, filled with nuggets and gentle reminders along the way that I still wanted to write. Oftentimes, ideas I had had for the big screen were the very ideas that eventually turned into award-winning films. Other times, it would be something as simple as a customer telling me I was a good writer, or people giving me positive feedback on a blog post I had written.

My point here is pretty simple: my decision not to pursue a career in writing immediately after college was due to a fear of rejection. While money is of course important in planning for one's future, anyone who truly believes in themselves lives by the mantra "Where there's a will, there's a way." And quite simply, although I believed in myself enough to "write my own paycheck" in sales, I did not believe in myself enough to forge my path as a writer. And it took me ten years to build the courage to write this book and start to really face these fears of rejection. Don't get me wrong: I am grateful that I work in sales and I plan to do it for many more years, but that is an outcome predicated somewhat on the luck that I fell into something I became passionate about.

All this to say, our fears of rejection are not always plain and obvious. It's not as simple as being scared to join a club soccer team or to walk up to a girl at the bar and say hello. Our fear of rejection lurks in the shadows when we do not chase our big dreams and go about our everyday lives feeling just good enough to get by, but not quite as happy as we would be if we decided to accept rejection as an everyday part of life. Of course, it is only through rejection and failure that we can ever really value success, so constantly running away from rejection is really just a way of prolonging the path to the proverbial mountaintop.

When it comes to picking a stranger up at the bar, I am no expert by any means. It has never really been my thing to approach strangers. I still face some fears and social anxieties in dedicated networking settings. That being said, there is one thing I do know about cold outreach, which is that cheesy or contrived openers never work. People see right through the nonsense. That is why approaching a stranger at a bar and asking "Do you come here often?" is perceived as cliché.

When it comes to facing your fears, you generally start by approaching them from a manageable angle. For example, you might be overwhelmed by the prospect of trying to run a marathon, especially if you do not have any substantial history with running. But you might rationalize your decision to start by telling yourself any number of things. You might tell yourself that this will be a process that involves setting miniature goals for yourself—3 miles, then 5 miles, then 10 miles, and so on— until you reach the ultimate goal of 26.2 miles, which is really no different than any other milestone you have reached in your life. You might tell yourself that you enjoy physical activity, so it stands to reason that you could come to appreciate running. You might even tell yourself that you enjoy listening to podcasts or music, and that running will give you an opportunity to be engaged with those things. Lastly, you could even justify your endeavor by remembering that you like being outside, and that running will force you to try to be more meditative generally in your life, reflecting on all of the ways that you can interact with the outdoors around you.

Whatever it is, you start generally by acclimating yourself to the situation by establishing some sort of connection between you and the thing that you fear. This is probably how we came up with sayings like "dip your toe in the water," or "wading from the shallow end into the deep end." Indeed, when you are a child learning how to swim, you move gradually from the shallow end with your floaties on, into the deep end, where eventually you learn to stay by treading water without floaties.

Trying to connect with another human being is really no different. We all learn to adopt certain values around which we build our entire lives. Suffice it to say, these values mean a lot to us. Trust is built with others when we find that they share the same values as us. I gave an example in Chapter 2 about who you would entrust to babysit your child: a charismatic sales guy who takes you out for fun client entertainment events, or your best friend (or a family member). Generally speaking, people are more likely to choose the latter. And that is because you naturally surround yourself with people who share your values. And quite simply, you trust people who share your values more than you trust people who do not—even if the people who do not share your values are more fun and entertaining.

What does this mean for cold outreach? It means we are best-served by discovering ways to connect with other people on an emotional level. When I reach out to a new prospect, I spend very little effort or time discussing what my product is or how it works. I focus almost all of my energy trying to understand who the person is and what we have in common. After all, if finding common ground with my fears is the way that I overcome them, it stands to reason that the same is true in reverse for people who are being approached by salespeople. It is not exactly comfortable to be approached by a stranger in most circumstances, so alleviating that fear by establishing common ground and values is crucial.

What I am going to do next is showcase my cold outreach system that I train all of our inside salespeople on. Once we have walked through that, I will bridge the gap between applying my system in a formal sales setting to applying my system in the day-to-day world. Even if you do not work in sales, understanding effective cold outreach is useful for pretty much any situation where you are looking to break the ice with another person.

Authentic & Eccentric Cold Outreach

Most formal sales training programs teach people to do the exact opposite of what they ought to do when reaching out to a customer for the first time. Simply by instructing someone to be different than they are, sales training programs remove the "humanness" of the interaction, which diminishes the chance of a response since we have already established that we must seek commonality. And humans have very little in common with robots. As I mentioned in Chapter 1, if you can train a human to do something, you can likely train a robot to do it, too. So acting like a robot means you will soon make yourself ripe for replacement by way of automation. This is not a good long-term outcome for any salesperson.

People are weird. All of us are eccentric in one way or another. I really hate the word "normal," because I don't even know what it means. It is completely subjective. To be sure, there are people we meet who seem to fall more outside of the proverbial norm that we are accustomed to. But that does not by default make them more or less interesting, or better people, than anyone else. Even people who seem fairly "normal" on paper almost certainly have some very interesting stories to tell you if you sat down and really asked them questions with sincerity. If they were willing to open up to you, it is likely that they have some of their own weird secrets: singing songs to their cat (I am guilty of this), having a routine for how they start and finish a shower (I am also guilty of this), or maybe even being fascinated by aliens (guilty as charged) or what is on the bottom of the ocean (you guessed it!).

The first thing I tell inside salespeople when I hire them is that I want them to embrace themselves and everything that makes them authentically weird. The weirder they are, the better. And whether or not you like my theory on weirdness, it is absolutely true today that most buyers are inundated with emails, many of which come from salespeople, vying for their attention. What this means is that you need to stand out from the pack. Hence, the weirder you are, the better. Even though Waldo was dressed in strange red and white attire, he was always hard to spot in those *Where's Waldo?* books because he wasn't weird enough to really stand out from the pack. And Waldo looked like a pretty weird guy. You need to be weirder than Waldo.

I compartmentalize a good sales email into three parts: The Excuse, The Value Proposition, and The Ask. We will dive into all three parts, but before we do, it is important that we talk about the goal. The goal in writing cold outreach to a new potential prospect is to get them interested enough to spend some time together to learn about the product that we sell. We have already established that attention spans are limited what with the excess of stimulus that most buyers already experience because of the sheer abundance of correspondence that they receive. This means that you must set micro-goals within the goal. And the micro-goal for each stage in your outreach is simply to get your prospective buyer to the next stage of your outreach.

What does this mean in the real world? It means that when I write a subject line for my e-mail, the goal is to get the person to open the e-mail. It is not to get that person to buy my product. It is simply to get them to open the message. Generally speaking, sales-y messages like "Act now! Supply limited" or "How we can increase productivity by 300% with my product" are not great openers. Why is that? Well, we discussed in Chapter 1 how people grow to become aware of when someone is selling them something. And these types of subject lines are the types of subjects buyers have seen their entire lives from the brands who are selling to them. Their first instinct is to think "This is a sales email" rather than "This is a human being." Put this book down right now and open up your e-mail inbox. Unless you are compulsive like me and check your email constantly, you probably have a bunch of marketing e-mails from brands whose e-mail lists you have wound up on. Look at the subject line of all of those e-mails. Chances are, you probably delete most of these. So there you go, you just learned a lesson: don't use subject lines that look like the ones you are now about to delete from your inbox.

Here are some better examples of subject lines that are hard to ignore:

"Hello from a fellow alumnus of X University"

"Hello from a fan of [buyer's product company name]"

"Fellow Boston Bruins fan looking to connect"

Or, perhaps for a Star Wars fan, "Read or read not, there is no try"

You get the picture. You are using something appealing to your target to establish some mutual synergy. And from there, the goal remains the same. The goal of the first sentence is to get the reader to the second sentence. The goal of the second sentence is to get the reader to the third sentence. The goal of each and every word is to get the reader to the next word. And eventually, as you will soon see, the ultimate goal at the end is to have mutual agreement to meet together. But it is only the sum of the parts—the e-mail in its entirety—which should convince the reader that this is a worthy outcome.

None of this can be accomplished if you are writing an essay to the client. Most people feel out whether or not they have the time to read an email by staring at its sheer size once they open it. If the email is too long, it is likely to get deleted, even if the email itself is some of the finest prose ever known to mankind. This is really no different than how you would approach the proverbial stranger at the bar. If you went up to them and told them your life story, they are likely to be a little creeped out. But, if you led off with something short and sweet about a commonality, it leaves the door open for curiosity that can spark a conversation.

Without further ado, let's start to dive into the structure of sound cold outreach.

Part 1: The Excuse

I call the first part of cold outreach "the excuse" because you are always interrupting someone's day, and when you interrupt someone's day, you better have a good excuse. You would never walk up to someone, for example, who is clearly on a phone call, and ask them for directions. If you did, you would at least preface your statement with a good excuse: "Hey, I know you look really busy but this is kind of an emergency so I hope you don't mind me interrupting you to ask a quick question?" Anything short of that and the person who you are calling upon for help is likely to leave with a bad taste in their mouth over your poor manners, and this makes them all the more likely to decline helping you or to provide you with bad directions. No one wins in that situation.

The excuse for reaching out to someone should always be something personal. Most sales training programs miss this, encouraging the sales rep to open up with some sort of before and after scenario. This could be something about how bad life is today in the absence of the product that is being sold, and what life looks like after, followed by examples of satisfied customers and some statistics to substantiate the point. While none of this is objectively wrong to do, per se, it is also what pretty much everyone else is doing. And if you are fighting for someone's attention and every single vendor is promising them a better outcome, ultimately it all just starts to sound like white noise.

Here are some examples of successful outreach I have performed.

I found someone who, like me, was an English major in college. She happened to go to The University of North Carolina. Anyone who goes to UNC hates Duke University as they are bitter in-state sports rivals. As a fellow English major myself, I penned an email to this prospect with the subject line "Hello from a fellow English major and Duke hater." I opened the email by lamenting how everyone told me I would never get a job out of college with my useless English degree and how it was serendipitous for us to find ourselves linking up in the world, both gainfully employed, with me trying to sell her my product. I went on to talk about how we must also have a mutual disdain for Duke. Let's face it, Duke resembles the New England Patriots in many ways, in that everyone who is not a fan of either team generally has a lot of ill-will toward their fanbases. And this is coming from a diehard Patriots fan. It's just reality.

The prospect I was writing to wrote back to me saying that the email was clever and that she was interested in connecting with me. Meanwhile, I had only spent one or two sentences in the email getting to the meat and potatoes of what we were even selling—and even then, I left it all in high-level terminology. The point being, it did not really matter exactly "what" it was that I was selling—it was the "why" that is always more compelling. And in this case, the "why" was this commonality we had developed which might lead to some building of trust. From a point of trust, no matter what you are buying, you can at least assume that the seller is going to do everything they can to make sure you are successful. Here is the actual email:

Hey [Prospect],

Couple things...

1. Real happy to see a fellow English major thriving in the workforce! They always told me my degree wouldn't be worth much unless I became a teacher, turns out I am saving lives one at a time by selling fraud prevention and call authentication technology.

2. Duke stinks so it's great you did all of this at UNC.

In all seriousness, you look like the person who would vet technology for authenticating inbound callers. I know you guys do some stuff with [our competitor], but we would love to have an opportunity to show how we could augment those efforts. Let me know if you would be open to connecting sometime.

Cheers,

Jeff

There is something important I want to call out about this. Nowhere in this email did I compromise my authenticity. I really was an English major in college, I really do enjoy meeting people who shared my major, I genuinely do enjoy joking about us both being gainfully employed, and I also authentically hate Duke (N.B.—apologies to any Duke alumni/alumnae reading this). So nowhere did I sell my soul by writing this message. And this is the thing that is so hard for people to realize in today's politically-charged climate: you have so much more in common with most people than you would think. If you could only spend a little bit of time peeling the onion, chances are that you would have so much to talk about and agree on if you could get over the obvious differences you see at surface level. It is just a matter of finding out what those commonalities are so you can exploit them and turn them into a positive for both sides. Remember when we talked about empathy a couple chapters ago? You're going to need that to be able to get far enough with people to realize what values you share. It is those who lack empathy and write other people off entirely that do not even give themselves (and others) an opportunity to see what values they share.

Another favorite example of mine is a message I wrote to American Airlines about seven years ago. I will need the reader to reserve their judgment for the story. Ready? Ok, now that you have cast your judgment aside, we can dive in. I set up a Twitter account for my cat, Zoe, nearly a decade ago. It was mainly a joke and "Zoe" would tweet about her Fancy Feast cravings and how absurd it was that I was traveling so much for work and leaving her home alone. "Zoe" eventually had a

very funny back-and-forth dialogue with American Airlines on
Twitter:

This interaction was one of many between my cat and the
largest airline on the planet. A lot of my friends thought it was
really funny, and Fancy Feast actually caught wind of it and sent
Zoe a bunch of free cans of food (which is a story for another day).
Clearly, whoever was in charge of the airline's social media at the
time deserved a lot of credit for the whimsical way in which they
interacted with customers. Anyway, I used this when reaching

out to American Airlines because it was actually one of the reasons that I viewed their brand in a positive light and I thought it was important for them to understand that in my outreach:

Subject: American Airlines Tweets With My Cat

"Hi AA,

Hope you had a good weekend. I want to laud you and your social media team as I have had several fun interactions with them on Twitter. Most memorably, many of my friends loved an exchange last year between AA and my cat (don't judge me), some of which I have attached to this e-mail.

I am reaching out because I moved to NYC last week to start a job with [my company]. We pre-identify callers who reach your Customer Service lines, saving you over 50 cents and 30-60 seconds on every phone call. With the call volume AA receives, this will add up to millions of dollars of savings, shorter hold times, happier customers, and happier agents.

In spite of my weird cat story, I am wondering if you would be interested in meeting to learn more about [my company]. I am a fellow soccer fan, looking to make the trek to Brazil this summer, and if we can chat, I will return the favor by booking my flight with AA :)"

As with the first e-mail, everything I sent to this person was completely sincere. I am a very loyal frequent flyer of American Airlines, I really did have this weird story about my cat and their social media team, and I really am a big soccer fan who has been wanting to go to the World Cup as a bucket list item for quite some time. This authenticity is palpable, and surely enough, the individual set up a meeting with me—presumably because I had taken the time and the initiative to try to connect on a deeper level beyond just selling my widget.

I will go ahead and share a few other ideas and examples that worked. I distinctly remember many years ago getting a meeting with OpenTable, a company that allows you to book restaurant reservations online. My e-mail was about how I was angry that my ex-girlfriend had broken up with me and got to keep all of the OpenTable points we had earned together. I recommended that they install a "break-up" feature to avoid situations like this. It was obvious that I was joking in my e-mail (although, it's not an *awful* idea, after all), and the recipient of the e-mail found it so funny and endearing that she took me up on a meeting. Perhaps Larry David might like this idea for an episode of *Curb Your Enthusiasm*.

Another time, I wrote to a senior executive for a Fortune 500 retailer who went to Auburn University. This might be a baseless stereotype, but I assumed that anyone who has anything to do with Auburn University cares about Auburn football. There was a famous game nearly a decade ago when Auburn played Alabama in what is called "The Iron Bowl." It is one of the most fierce rivalries in all of sports. Anyway, Alabama lined up to kick a field goal, and because the field goal fell short, an Auburn player caught it and then ran over 100 yards to score a game-winning touchdown. This type of thing almost never happens. When I saw that my prospect was an

Auburn grad, my excuse was pretty simple: "I know you get a lot of these emails, so let me start by re-living the most special moment of your life with you." In that sentence, I linked to a video of that very special play. Surely enough, the prospect was so amused that he wrote back almost instantly putting me in touch with the right member of his team to facilitate a conversation.

I will shamefully admit an example of where someone went too far in adopting my methodology. I once had an overzealous sales rep whom we will call Daniel. Daniel once wrote to a prospect under the premonition that the prospect was a St. Louis Cardinals fan, and Daniel said that he, too, was a fan of the Cardinals. The prospect actually looked up Daniel's Facebook profile and saw him wearing a Red Sox hat, which all but assured him that Daniel was lying. Unfortunately, this was only the tip of the iceberg. Daniel once wrote to another prospect with an "excuse" that he had survived a disease. Turns out that Daniel was not actually a survivor of that disease. This is obviously one of the most insensitive things that someone could do, and nothing I would ever condone (I didn't). Being disingenuous is not part of the philosophy, especially when there are so many other ways to try to connect with someone on a personal level.

While we are on the subject of St. Louis sports teams, let me go ahead and give you a much better example of someone executing this strategy on my team. This actually happened quite recently. My team rep and I discovered that our prospect was a die-hard St. Louis Blues hockey fan through one of his interests on LinkedIn. There is a website called Cameo that allows you to book shout-outs from celebrities and other public figures for a fee. It turns out that the P.A. announcer for the St. Louis Blues does cameos on the website for a modest fee. We paid twenty bucks or so for him to make a video for our prospect. The video was about three minutes in length, and in it, the P.A. announcer talked about his love for the St. Louis Blues, before talking about what my company does and why the prospect should take a meeting with us. As you can probably guess, there was no hesitation on the side of the customer to take a meeting with us as we had clearly done our research in an attempt to connect with him. I will admit, however, as a Boston Bruins fan who was in the crowd watching my favorite team lose in person in Game 7 of the Stanley Cup Finals against the St. Louis Blues just a year prior, it did hurt me a little to bless the cameo.

Another example of a good excuse to reach out to someone is based on content that they have written. I once uncovered the personal blog of a prospect of mine called "The Traveling Parent." The blog was basically about how this man balanced his work life with his home life. As you can guess by the title of the blog, he traveled a lot for work and rarely saw his children. He had to get creative about using technology to stay in touch with them, and when he was at home, he needed to set certain boundaries in order to maximize his time with his children. I was actually personally touched while reading his blog. And even though I am not a parent, I do travel quite a bit for work and I could really empathize with his struggle through my own personal experiences of feeling homesick whenever I would hit the road for a new destination. I wrote him a message saying as much after dozens of failed attempts to connect with him previously, and surely enough, he wrote back to me with an interest in meeting. In this scenario, it was by making myself vulnerable that I showed him my humanity, and he responded in kind.

Content that people write is ripe for good, genuine connections. A personal blog is one thing, but oftentimes people are also writing professionally about subject matter that is relevant to their work, or even for volunteer work that they do in their personal time. For example, I am a volunteer in the Big Brother Big Sister program. People who participate in that program have a dedication to mentorship and serving underrepresented communities. That alone is a great reason for connecting with someone who participates in the same program or has undertaken any other sort of commitment to mentorship in their lives. Or if that individual has contributed thought leadership for a publication like the Harvard Business Review, you might find some meaning in what they had to say and explain to them why it resonated with you and why it makes you hopeful that a conversation could be mutually beneficial.

We established earlier that I am a die-hard Boston Bruins fan. That much can be gleaned simply by finding my Twitter bio online, but also in several other places if you dig deep enough. The best outreach I ever received was from a sales rep at a company called Gong. I did not have a particular need for their product but I took the meeting with them simply because the outreach was so clever. That is what good outreach does: it makes the buyer forget whether or not they are even interested in the product, because they are more interested in meeting with you. For the sake of example, I have shared this outreach below:

Subject: A Team Full of David Pastrnaks

Hi Jeff,

As a VP and a Bruins fan, I'm sure you can appreciate the hours top players put in behind the scenes watching game-film to perfect their game and gain a leg up on their opponents.

When it comes to sales, it's not so different. Visibility into your team's customer-facing conversations can gauge accountability to messaging, competitive differentiation, qualification, etc., ensuring reps are consistently delivering leads that bring the sales org to target -- cause your reps all want to have a sales hat trick like Pastrnak.

Can I grab 15 minutes of your time tomorrow or Monday to unpack how leaders like yourself partner with Gong to drive consistency across teams?

P.S. I'm a Sharks fan, so I hope to see you guys in the Stanley Cups finals.

This message hits the nail on the head with my formula in every possible way. As a Bruins fan, there is no way I am ignoring a subject line that includes the name of the best player on the team. What I also like is the rep managed to make her case for her product while still using hockey terminology and lingo that made her hockey theme seem like it was not a throw-away just to get my attention (more on that when we cover the value proposition in a little bit). Lastly, she shared that she is a Sharks fan, which signals to me that we actually do have a common interest in hockey, and that she is not just using something about me to manipulate me into a meeting.

Even non-personal excuses can work if they establish some sort of commonality between you and the person you are trying to work with. In any industry, there are going to be new trends, thought leadership, and so on. A simple way to get through to someone is to reach out to let them know about one of these trends and why that trend makes it logical for you and the prospect to get together for a conversation. In this scenario, at bare minimum you are adding some value to the customer by giving them information about their industry they might not have otherwise known, and you are casually reminding them that you two both play in the same sandbox. You could even play off of current events that are universally viewed in a certain light. For example, almost everyone agreed that the first Presidential Debate of 2020 was an absolute nightmare to watch, no matter who you were rooting for. An e-mail the following day with the subject, "because last night was a disaster..." would probably go well with almost any prospect.

Establishing commonality works because succinctly, we are emotional creatures and we make decisions based on our emotions. The reason our best friends are our best friends is presumably because we share certain things in common, be it our values or interests or both. When people see you for who you really are, they are much more likely to want to get to know you than when you pretend to be someone you are not. Yes, if you are really, really good at pretending to be someone you are not, then you might get away with a lack of authenticity. But that would also suggest to me that you are living a life of lies. I am of the opinion that most people can sniff through insincerity fairly easily. And if being your authentic self also involves being self-deprecating and acknowledging your flaws, then you are all the more human like your prospect. In fact, one reason why we find so many of our favorite comedians to be so funny is because of the ways they make fun of themselves. We find that to be real, authentic, and relatable, and because of its relatability, therein lies the humor.

What does the excuse have to do with picking up someone at a bar? You are asking the wrong guy because I told you that it is not my forté. But if I were to guess, it would involve understanding something about a person and being able to articulate pretty plainly why you admire that thing. Telling someone they are beautiful or handsome is flattering but it is also something anyone else could tell that individual without necessarily tying it back to any sort of commonality between them and the individual they are complimenting. Idolatry is not the same thing as commonality. After all, if you are going to interrupt someone's evening, you better have a good excuse. I remember when I was in college, I had a crush on a girl who had the "Autism Speaks" logo tattooed on her shoulder. I told her that I really liked the tattoo because I had spent some time when I was younger and even during college fundraising for cures to autism. I remember that she was very touched by that, and she explained to me that her brother had autism. She never became my girlfriend, and that was probably a function of my shyness more than anything else, but it's no matter. I still feel good knowing that I touched her life in some small way, because the reason I told her I liked the tattoo to begin with was related to the common interest we appeared to share.

Now, it is one thing to have a good excuse to reach out to someone and to share that with them. But once you have made your excuse, you need to have a compelling reason why you merit their attention. And that is where the Value Proposition comes in.

#2: The Value Proposition

A value proposition is exactly what it sounds like—the proposed value that you are bringing to a prospect. The best value proposition should really be short and sweet. You often hear the term "elevator pitch" and you see competitions where people have to give elevator pitches in a very short amount of time. This is intentional. If you are unable to explain what value you can add succinctly, it probably means that the value you add is nebulous or confusing, because otherwise it would be easy to explain. Moreover, people have short attention spans, so you really need to cut to the chase when explaining what value you can offer.

First though, let's make sure we do not make the most common mistake that I have had to correct within my own ranks. A huge mistake that I often see is people getting so wrapped up in their "excuse" to reach out, that they forget about it for the rest of the email. They might say something like this:

"Dear So and So,

Your recent article on the bureaucracy of procurement processes really caught my attention because I have long held the same beliefs. Thank you for being a voice of reason. I particularly liked the part where you called out how the best vendors are often not selected as a result of this bureaucracy.

I am reaching out to you because you are the Head of Procurement at XZY Company. We sell a product that eases the burden of onboarding new vendors.

Let me know if you are open to catching up next week to brainstorm about this.

Sincerely,

Learning Sales Rep"

If you cannot spot what is wrong with this message, that is because it is quite subtle: there is no connection between the first and second paragraphs. The writer goes from discussing an article to immediately explaining why they are reaching out to the person and what they are trying to sell to them. It almost makes the first paragraph look disingenuous, because the "personal" part of the email is immediately discarded in lieu of a straight up sales pitch. Fortunately, it does not take much to fix this. It would be as simple as using this transitional sentence: "Because you seem very interested in figuring out ways to make the procurement process easier, I thought it would be a good idea for us to connect and brainstorm about our product, which does X, Y, and Z for you." As long as you are giving a reason why your excuse somehow ties to your value proposition, you are golden. But if you suddenly forget your excuse in the interest of jumping right into your pitch, it will leave the recipient wondering about the relevance of your excuse if not for anything other than to indicate you have some things in common, which might have nothing to do with the conversation the individual is trying to have with you.

With that being said, I do think the transitional sentence I proposed above is highly effective because it also subtly puts the reader in a position where saying "no" might not be in accordance with their stated goals. If someone has gone out of their way to publicly criticize a specific problem and you reach out to them stating that you are reaching out precisely because of their criticism, it puts the reader in a position where they feel compelled to respond. Certainly when I publish this book and then get bombarded by sales emails about authenticity, I would feel like a hypocrite to tell those salespeople to go pound sand. Working this type of language into your value proposition as a quasi-excuse or transition phrase can be a small but highly effective maneuver.

The scope of the value proposition depends largely on what you are selling and what industry you are in. For the last seven years, I have been selling into a very niche industry against just a couple of competitors. Generally speaking, my audience consists of people whose job largely revolves around understanding what vendor solutions are out there. My value proposition can be fairly high-level and straightforward—"we are one of the vendors doing this very niche thing and I do not believe we have had an opportunity to meet before, so let us know if we could connect."

Unfortunately, for most people it is not so simple. But that does not mean that the solution is much harder. My high-level thesis is that the value proposition should be 1-2 sentences, 3 at most, it should tie the excuse into it in some way, and it should speak mostly in terms of measurable outcomes or "whys." What are those?

Well, outcomes are fairly obvious. These are the things that happen for the customer when the customer buys your product. Measurable outcomes assign some sort of specificity to the outcome—like saying "we will triple your revenues" versus "we will increase your revenues." A "why" is actually not an outcome at all—it's just an explanation for why you and your company care about this problem and why you want to help. Why is the "why" important? For all of the reasons we have already discussed. People get onboard with ideas if they feel commonality with those who share the ideas. If you are selling a customer experience product to a customer experience professional, chances are, that customer experience professional is passionate about customer experience. What better way to establish commonality than to explain why you, too, care about customer experience?

Now that we have established how the Value Proposition

works, let's go back and re-work my email from a moment ago. Here is what it might look like now:

"Subject: Your article in Procurement Magazine

Dear So and So,

Your recent article on the bureaucracy of procurement processes really caught my attention because I have long held the same beliefs. Thank you for being a voice of reason. I particularly liked the part where you called out how the best vendors are often not selected as a result of this bureaucracy.

Since you are so passionate about innovation in the realm of procurement and making life easier for procurement professionals, I was interested in brainstorming with you over our new solution. We are seeing a 3x increase in efficiency in private betas for procurement professionals and it would be an honor to get your feedback.

Let me know if you are open to catching up next week to look at this.

Sincerely,

Improved Sales Rep"

This hits the formula perfectly: subject line that is impossible to ignore, establishing commonality, transitioning that commonality into a compelling value proposition with measurable outcomes, and an easy call to action.

#3: The Ask

Game of Thrones spoiler alert! Cover your eyes and ears if you have never watched it!

One of my favorite parts of the show was the very last episode when Bran Stark says, "Why do you think I came all this way?" It's a little funny coming from a pretty weird character who does not talk much. Succinctly, his character suffers a great deal in all the episodes leading up to the last one, but winds up in contention to have absolute power in the very end. He is telling everyone else around him that he did not go through this whole ordeal for nothing. The same is true for you in your cold outreach, although hopefully you suffer much less than Bran Stark.

If you went out of your way to approach a guy at the bar to tell him that you really liked his cologne, it would probably be a little creepy if you just walked away afterward. That is because when you go out of your way to establish some sort of commonality with a stranger, it seems bizarre if you do not establish anything with that commonality. Similarly, you would not email a prospect just to tell them you are both Boston Bruins fans. However, you might email a prospect to tell them you are both fans, and that you think it would be great to watch a game together sometime. This is "the ask."

Let's be honest—you are interrupting someone's day because you want something from them. To be fair, you must feel that they stand to benefit from spending time with you, too. You are not going to get that time unless you ask for it.

The ask is relatively simple compared to the other concepts we have covered in this chapter. Take a sentence and ask for whatever it is that you need. Because most conversations I have with customers are really brainstorming sessions, I like to use non-threatening language like "it would be great to brainstorm with you" or even the more 'sales-y' but still less threatening "let me know if I could introduce the concept to you." Regardless, I think one of the most important things you can do when asking for something is letting the person know that you are OK with them saying "no." It is often taught in sales trainings that you should not introduce objections to customers, and while I think that is often true, I don't see the harm in showing a customer that you are not going to be pushy. I like to close out many of my messages with something like this:

"Let me know if you are open to brainstorming on this idea with me next week. If it's not your cup of tea, I understand."

When it comes to the examples I have used in dating, I realize that my example above does not necessarily hold water. It can be a turnoff for people to appear to be lacking confidence. For example, you are unlikely to ask someone out on a date with the caveat that you would be understanding if they rejected you. But people that you ask on a date for the first time are oftentimes not people that you know very well. And quite frankly, if you did know them well, you would be likely to add the caveat, "I'd understand if you said no, because we are such good friends." Really, giving an "out" to someone is the same exact way you would treat a friend. You would not bully them into accepting your idea—you would let them know that your friendship will still be intact even if they disagree with you. The same is true here: ask for what you want but show the person that there is much more to life than whether or not they take you up on your offer.

One thing I really try to avoid in my cold outreach and really in all of my selling is looming deadlines. This is an artificially-imposed deadline on someone meeting a call to action. Generally speaking, looming deadlines hinge around pricing, e.g., "If you buy our product in the month of September, it will be half off." This is gimmicky because it is not authentic. It is gimmicky because it is what car salespeople do to you and honestly half of the promotional emails in your inbox—which we have established can be used as a rule for what **not** to do—are probably employing the same tactic. When you are having a serious conversation with a close friend or family member and recommending a certain course of action to them, you probably would not tell them they need to take your advice immediately or risk everything. Realistically, you would only do that if there was actually a compelling reason to do so. In traditional sales settings though, the looming deadlines you experience are rarely motivated by real timing hurdles. They are almost always motivated by someone who needs to bring a lot of revenue in the door at a certain time. When your favorite retailer has a sale, it is not because there is something about the given month that makes it more affordable to them to sell you clothes. It is because they know that offering you a looming deadline has an effect on human psychology.

Now, I know what you're thinking. Something like, "Jeff, you already told us you were an English major in college and that you know nothing about psychology. Why should I listen to you when every marketer in the world does this stuff?" Well, that is because people who market en masse are very different than people who market in unique business-to-business settings. If you work for a business-to-consumer company (think Amazon, or any large retail brand), looming deadlines will probably be effective for you, so go ahead and disregard my advice. However, if you sell large enterprise contracts like I do, the people you are dealing with are much more likely to see through your nonsense and feel that you are trying to rush a process that takes time. I recently moved forward with a vendor who offered me a looming deadline. I did not like that they had a deadline on their pricing, but they told me that they were raising money from investors and trying to bring in as much revenue as possible to help with their valuation. The more revenue they could show to the investors, the less dilution of their stock they would face. I believed them, and I signed up for their product. Surely enough, weeks later, they announced their Series B fundraising round. Here is the moral of the story: if you are going to use pressure tactics to try to bully someone into a sale, at least be genuine. I have been honest with my clients about why I ask for things when I ask for them so that they see that my demands are coming from a place of authenticity and that they are not borne out of just trying to close a deal. If people are made to feel in your outreach that any urgency you have is legitimate, they will act in kind. However, if they are made to feel like you're just trying to push them, they will also react in kind (i.e., not kindly) to that.

It is probably self-evident how these principles can be applied to everyday situations. My cold outreach method is useful when you are reaching out to anyone for the first time about anything it is that you desire. It could be valuable in reaching out about a potential job opportunity. It could be valuable in reaching out to a college admissions counselor. I suppose it could even be valuable for people who are looking for a better opening line on whatever dating app they use. But whether you are sitting behind a computer or not, the same principles hold true: try to remember the humanity of people around you and appreciate others for their own authenticity. Try to connect with them in a personal way and you will be pleasantly surprised by the results.

Now that you have the tools and the know-how to reach out cold from behind a computer, let's talk about how to reach out cold from behind a phone, and why it is so important to remember that everyone puts on their pants the same way.

Chapter 6

Cold Calling, or,
"How to Put on Your Pants"

When I was in high school, I got myself what at the time would have been considered a dream job as a member of the grounds crew for The Boston Red Sox. I spent my entire childhood obsessed with the Red Sox and baseball, and my dream was to become a professional baseball player. Unfortunately, baseball did not work out for me, so I resorted to a sales gig and writing books, but you can't win 'em all.

Anyway, the job on the grounds crew is always a fun story to tell people. Most people know about the grounds crew because they are the people who run out to put the tarp onto the field during a rain delay. Others are aware of the grounds crew because they clean up the base paths in between innings, and in some stadiums, members of the grounds crew even do dances as they do that work.

The reality, however, was that working on the grounds crew was just really hard work. What happened behind the scenes to make a baseball game happen every day was nothing short of remarkable. For a 7pm game, I was expected to be at the stadium at 7am to begin my work. I had a long commute, so I was up at 5am in the mornings over the summer in order to get to the stadium on time. While I did not work during many of the games, sometimes I did, which meant that my work days were sometimes as long as 15 or 16 hours with another turnaround the next morning to be back.

The work itself to get the field "game-ready" is pretty long and arduous. I would spend the first hour or two every morning with a wheelbarrow, a rake, and a shovel, circling the dirt warning track around the entire field cleaning up debris like peanut shells and beer cups. Nota bene: this is not a fun responsibility. When I was done, one of my next jobs would be to hose down the dugouts that were littered with sunflower seeds, tobacco, and Gatorade cups, using a squeegee to dry up the mess. The dugouts and bullpens both have bathrooms, and let's just say that

Major League Baseball players are not very clean during games. The bullpens needed a similar type of treatment, bases needed to be scrubbed of their dirt, trash runs needed to be made, and grass needed to be clipped. In the midst of summer, this was hard labor and was not a glorious job by any stretch of the imagination. Not to mention that Fenway Park is one of the oldest and most decrepit stadiums in the United States, so it was not uncommon to see rats running amok. To boot, I was making minimum wage and working on an hourly basis. That is when I really started to appreciate the value of money. Once the euphoria of working at Fenway Park had worn off, I was left with the hangover—that this was a really difficult and demanding job with few rewards.

A couple things we were always told were not to steal memorabilia from the stadium and not to initiate conversation with any of the players. Being the goody two-shoes that I was, I always observed these rules. That does not mean I did not have any cool stories. I distinctly remember cleaning the runway between the visitor's clubhouse and the visiting dugout when Hall of Famer Frank Robinson was walking through, and he stopped to thank me for my work and told me I was doing a good job. Another time, Hall of Famer (and hated Yankee) Derek Jeter thanked me and a few of my colleagues during the pregame warmups as we were hosing down the infield. And yet another time, I remember sitting next to Red Sox outfielder Coco Crisp during a rain delay, during which time he decided to regale me about his penchant for plus-sized women.

The reason I am telling you all this is to set the stage for a time I distinctly remember being shy and a lesson I learned about it shortly thereafter. The Red Sox used to have an excellent pitcher named Jonathan Papelbon, who would eventually become their closer and a World Series Champion with the team in 2011. On July 31, 2005, Papelbon made his major league debut as a starting pitcher. I watched the game from the roof deck in Fenway Park with my cousin because as a red Sox employee, I was allowed to go to any game that I wanted to go to. There had been much brouhaha and anticipation about this young pitcher, so the very next morning, I found myself in a strange predicament as I was doing my morning routine of picking up peanut shells around the outskirts of the stadium, when a young Papelbon was doing laps jogging around the same periphery.

Every few minutes, Papelbon would pass by me where I was doing my work, and every time he approached me, I wanted to turn to him and say, "Nice job yesterday." While it was technically breaking the rules, others on the staff had done similar such things all the time without repercussion and it would not have really been a big deal for me to have said something. And yet I found myself getting cold feet every time he passed by me. I had convinced myself that we were somehow on two different 'playing fields', since I was a high school kid raking up peanut shells and he was a professional athlete. I did not think of the 99% of scenarios where my kind remark would be warmly received and instead focused on the 1% likelihood that I would get rejected or that saying something would somehow backfire on me, convincing myself in that moment that that was actually the more likely scenario that would happen. For the entirety of that morning as I raked up the peanut shells and well into the evening, I tormented myself with the regret I felt for not having the courage to say a simple thing to an absolute stranger who I admired.

Not too long after that day, I found myself working a game with my peers on the grounds crew. The people I worked with were mostly college-aged interns studying turf science at large state universities throughout the Midwest. In some ways, I looked up to some of these kids because they were older than me. I remember telling one of them who was sitting next to me about how I was too shy to say hello to Jonathan Papelbon only a few days before. He was incredulous at the idea that I found it so difficult to simply congratulate someone on an achievement. He turned to me and said, "You realize he puts his pants on the same way you do, right?"

To seventeen-year-old me, this was actually kind of a novel idea. I had spent my entire childhood idolizing professional athletes, collecting and trading baseball cards. Every time I had gone to a Red Sox game as a child, I brought my glove with me and made my dad take me early so I could lean over the side of the dugout and try to collect as many autographs as possible. To this day, I still have a box of baseballs and other memorabilia that are signed by baseball players, and I don't even know any more who half the signatures belong to. At one point in my life, I had made sure to cover every single game in an entire season either watching them on TV or listening to them on the radio. I had always viewed baseball players as superheroes, not everyday people who put their pants on the same way as me. And I guess that attitude persisted late into my teenage years.

As for my colleague who provided me with the revelation—I forget what I said to him. I probably shrugged it off for fear of looking like a loser. But I will never forget that simple truth: we all put our pants on the same way. It is a simple way of saying that we are not as different as we might outwardly appear.

This is an essential truth when it comes to the idea of cold calling, or really any other moment in your life that involves interrupting someone else's day. Whether it is trying to approach an attractive stranger, trying to make a new friend at a networking or social event, or simply asking for directions, we are often confronted with moments in our lives where we need to make a decision between doing something uncomfortable with another human being, or deciding to do nothing at all out of fear.

Now, let's face it: nobody really enjoys cold calling. For one thing, it is tedious to pick up a phone all day and call people you do not know. More so, people get really worked up about the idea of being rejected. In fact, what we tend to fear the most is having our feelings hurt not only by the rejection itself, but also by the very real possibility that the person answering the phone may vilify us in the process. I remember several years ago a prospect I called on the phone infantilized me on a cold call by making me repeat phrases after him in an attempt to put me down and discourage me from calling him again. At that time in my career, it was debilitating enough for me that it ruined my entire day. Indeed, I have mentored young salespeople who have been treated like dirt by prospects in their cold outreach over the phone or via email, sometimes getting yelled at before they are hung up on. Each and every time this happens, they would take it personally. And while my advice of course is to never feel that way, I still understand why they do. We all get upset when this type of thing happens in our daily lives.

Eventually what starts to happen though is that you come to realize that it is the other person who should be embarrassed in these scenarios, not you. I once had a rep for whom English was a second language, and a prospect actually criticized his English. Of course, this is entirely unprofessional, and I dealt with that matter on behalf of my rep by escalating that up the food chain within the organization of the prospect so as to ensure that his biased behavior would not continue. As for my rep, I had this to say: "You're a college student going out on a limb and you know not to behave like that. The person who said this to you is an adult and working professional who did something they should not have done. He is the one who should be embarrassed, not you." I said that and I generally say this type of thing whenever it is relevant because it is true, and it tends to make people feel better when they realize the power of this truth. When other people are rude to you, your natural inclination is to one-up them because your feelings are hurt. There is a quiet power in remaining silent and knowing for yourself that you have the upper hand by being unaffected by boorish behavior.

I can only speak in generalities here, but I have found that the people who go above and beyond to be rude are people who tend not to matter much. For example, I have never called on a C-Level executive at a Fortune 500 company and had them treat me like a plebeian. I have, however, called on low-level people at smaller institutions who go out of their way to feel insulted by the mere idea that someone might be selling them something and then go further out of their way to make sure that I feel doubly insulted and personally attacked. The best thing to do there is always to let it go. What I tell myself is that for someone to act that way, they must lead a miserable life. There is no other explanation as to what would drive someone to demean another human being they do not know, other than to say that they are so unhappy personally that they can only find joy in bringing others down to their sad state of existence. Either that, or they are just having a bad day. Whichever one it is, neither scenario leads to you or me actually being bad people. After all, how could a complete stranger know enough about us to make such judgments?

All this to say, between my story about how we put our pants on the same way, and the reality that even in the worst case scenario there is absolutely nothing wrong with you (unless you are a liar or a pushy person—don't be those things), what do you have to lose by taking a chance and cold calling? What do you have to lose asking someone out that you have a crush on? If you do not have any friends, what do you have to lose by signing up to join a recreational adult soccer league? I have been this person in all of these scenarios. I once was nervous about making cold calls, but now I do it every day. I once freaked out about every single message a crush might be sending me, trying to unpack all of its meaning. Now I am just forthright and direct with people and I hope for the best. When I moved to New York City, I was lonely and I had few friends nearby. Then I stopped feeling sorry for myself and joined a Mixed Martial Arts gym, a recreational soccer league, and filled up my schedule with various other activities. Have I stumbled upon the way? Sure. I have had people hang up on me, I have ruined friendships I had by revealing my feelings, and I have failed sometimes in making new friends. But I do not regret any of these decisions. I would rather live my life knowing that I tried to do all the things I wanted to do and succeeded most of the time rather than doing nothing at all for fear of not succeeding one hundred percent of the time. I suppose this is the simple way of articulating what Wayne Gretzky once said, "You miss 100 percent of the shots that you don't take."

This is the mentality that anyone needs to adopt when they take on cold-calling. Whoever you are calling—whether they are the CEO of a Fortune 500 company or some low-level person at a smaller company—they put on their pants the same way that you do. They are human beings with all sorts of problems. No matter how much money they make or how powerful they are, they have problems. They might just have different problems than the ones that you have. So treat them like human beings with human problems. A person's worth is not determined by their job title or how much money they make. For most people, worth is decided by their character or even more simply, their ability to find happiness. Here is my advice, and you can probably already guess what it is.

My advice is to bring authenticity into your cold calling by treating the person like they are just any other person you would like to be friends with. This means you do not put them on a pedestal when they are a high-ranking big shot, and you also do not speak down to them if they are someone without decision-making capability at a smaller organization. You have a solution to give them that will presumably help them, and for that, you should be genuinely interested in wanting to connect with them to help make a difference in their lives, provided that is something you actually care about. Though I will say, the saying "It is better to give than it is to receive," does not come from nowhere—it comes

from our innate desire to touch the lives of others. So bring that
to your conversation.

What this means in practice is actually quite simple. I see
most salespeople coming into their cold-calling with a script. Presumably this is because they are nervous about calling people and
want to make sure they do not slip up. Or perhaps it is because
they suspect they will not have much time or might be rushed off
the phone, so they want to make sure they get out all of their key
points. The issue with all of this is that it is pretty easy to know
when someone is reading from a script. When you hear people
rattling off certain buzzwords, for example, it sounds a little bit
corny, and you can tell the difference between what normal, off-
the-cuff conversation sounds like versus a scripted conversation.
And as we discussed back in Chapter 1, we are hard-wired to
identify when we are being "sold" to. It is really important not to
give off that robotic vibe.

Instead, act with some self-awareness. First of all, you are
interrupting someone's day. So act like it. If you were lost and you
needed directions, you would not just approach a stranger and ask
for directions. That would be a little bit presumptuous and rude.
You would instead make an excuse for interrupting their day. You
might say something like "Hey stranger, I am really sorry to bug
you, but I do not live here and I am lost. I was hoping you might
help me with some directions." Your honesty here shows that you
are a thoughtful person who does not take someone else's time
for granted. The context about how you are feeling shows the
stranger that you are just like them, in that you, too, have certain
fears and doubts that they can almost certainly relate to. Under
this pretext, a stranger will be much more willing to help you out

with directions than if you were to just interrupt their day, tap them on the shoulder, and demand their help.

When I cold call someone, the first thing I do is acknowledge that I am calling them out of the blue and that I know I am interrupting their day. I do that because that is the same thing I do virtually any other time I disrupt the day of another human being. It is the protocol through which we all mutually agree we should operate. Why is it any different in a sales setting? This opening salvo is actually disarming because the self-awareness either consciously or sub-consciously signals to the buyer that you are not presumptuous about their time or their desire to speak with you, and I think it also is likely to come across as genuine versus the alternative of diving straight into some rehearsed elevator pitch.

What I also avoid in my cold calling is any language I would not normally use when talking to a friend. For example, I don't say things like, "I would love to find a mutually beneficial time for us to connect." That sounds lame. Would you approach a stranger at a bar, compliment their shoes, and ask if there is a mutually beneficial time to connect for a date in the future? Unless you are a real nerd, probably not (but if you are a real nerd, please take no offense, and do what makes you happy). I also don't talk about work I do with the prospect's competitor. If someone approached you at a bar to ask you on a date and mentioned that they were also friends with a few of your exes, would you be more or less excited about the date? I suppose I am a little worried about how some people might answer this question, but my guess is that an overwhelming majority would find this information to be a turnoff. Long story short, talk to people in a cold call the same way you would talk to anyone when you were trying to introduce some sort of relationship to them the first time. That starts by being genuine. Keep it high level, approachable, cut to the chase, and ask point blank whether or not they want to meet. I realize I am making it sound pretty simple, but it really is that easy, and the more that you overthink it, the more likely you are to end up speaking like a robot. And one day, you will be replaced by the robots as a result, because the robots will be just as good as you are at listing off the bullet points about what makes your product worth looking into.

I realize that simplifying a cold call in this way might not be satisfying to everyday sales practitioners who are looking for actionable advice on their day-to-day activities. So let's dig into this a little bit deeper.

It is obvious by now that my philosophy is going to be around preserving authenticity around your interaction with a prospect in a cold call. An obvious difference between a cold call and most everyday scenarios is that you are behind a telephone and not face-to-face with someone. This naturally means that there will be some slight differences between how you would behave in the cold call versus how you might approach a stranger in real life. The most apparent difference is that behind the telephone, no one will know who is calling them until you tell them who it is. So, as is customary, you should start out by introducing who you are. I have learned about strategies where people start off by saying something (anything) else. This is a terrible idea. It is a terrible idea because when your day is interrupted by a phone call you do not recognize, you generally want to know right away who is calling you. You certainly do not want some creative distraction. In this way, the approach is very different from a cold e-mail. Why is that? Well, in a cold e-mail, you have the time to read through it at your leisure. On a cold call, everything is happening in real-time. Your patience is much thinner as the recipient of a cold call than it is as the recipient of a cold e-mail. However, where it might be more successful to deploy a strategy where you lead off with creativity is in leaving a voicemail, because most voice-mails sound pretty generic, so in the spirit of standing out (as we learned in the cold e-mailing chapter), it may actually behoove you to start with something unusual in a voicemail. Similar to an e-mail, a voicemail can be consumed on someone's own time. In a real-life conversation, however, there is a high likelihood of such behavior coming across as contrived, especially in a much more rushed setting.

Once I have introduced myself, I acknowledge that I am interrupting the day of the person I am calling. This means I need an excuse. Here is the thing though—I try not to have too many rules here. Because authentically in real life, the way you approach different people will vary on the situation. Sometimes I might have enough information about a prospect to know we have a lot in common. When that is the case, I might try to lead off by disarming them with some values that I know we share. More often than not, whatever "excuse" I have for disturbing their day is usually professional more than personal. Either way, it needs to be brief so you can dig right into why you are calling. I try to keep this very high level and avoid buzzwords. What are buzzwords? Phrases like "ROI" or "machine learning" or "saving time and money." As in most things, I try to avoid getting too deep into the "what" and get more into the "why." After all, the person you are calling is interested in solving some sort of problem. Signaling your interest in their values is much better than telling them about whatever widget you have. Their interest in the widget you are selling hinges on why you built it anyway.

They say half the battle when you want to lose weight is just showing up at the gym. The same is true for cold-calling: half the battle is just picking up the phone. Be a normal human, apologize for interrupting someone's day, get right into the "why," and ask for something.

Chapter 7

Objection Handling & Saying "Yes" Before "Yes!"

This is exactly what we
need to solve our biggest issue.

There is a saying that I always liked: "The sale starts at 'No'." Why is that? Well, anyone can sit there and take an order. We established in Chapter 1 that the coming wave of artificial

Chapter 7

Objection Handling & Saying "Yes" Before "Yes!"

There is a saying that I always liked: "The sale starts at 'No'." Why is that? Well, anyone can sit there and take an order. We established in Chapter 1 that the coming wave of artificial

121

intelligence jeopardizes the need for salespeople. Already, there are chatbots answering questions on websites instead of inbound sales development teams. It is pretty easy to hire someone or deploy technology to take "yes" for an answer. What is much more challenging is overcoming a "no." That is where the human element can really come in.

They also say that the best defense is a good offense. This is a phrase that is often applied to sports and military combat, with the idea that you cannot be scored on when you are on the offensive. The same is true for selling: you can actually avoid much of the objections altogether—which I would liken to "playing defense"—if you get out ahead of them and establish what "Yes" would look like. I call this idea "Making the customer say 'yes' before they say 'yes.'"

Before I start launching into examples of what I mean by that, we first need to establish what needs to happen in order to generate a sale. It is actually a pretty simple formula with two parts.

The first part of the formula is identifying a pain. This is establishing that the customer has a problem that they would like to fix. Sometimes the pain is obvious. When you have a toothache, you know that you need to go to the dentist. Similarly, in your work, you might have certain goals and initiatives that surface around perceived areas of weakness. So your team decides to solve a problem and naturally considers looking at vendor solutions in order to do so. This happens all the time and it is fairly evident when it is the case. But sometimes pain is not very obvious. When you have a toothache it is one thing, but you might have a cavity and never realize it until you go to the dentist. And that type of pain also surfaces in the workplace. When the cable company's call center is flooded with calls because people are confused about their bill, the cable company might react by assuming that they have 'a pain' in their call center that they need to address. The reality is that the real pain has to do with transparency in how they communicate their billing to customers. There are instances where people are keenly aware of their own pain, and there are instances where people need to be shown that they have a pain that they were previously unfamiliar with.

The second part of the formula is establishing that your solution can deliver on the promise of fixing the pain. If you have a toothache or a cavity, your dentist will need to show you that applying a gel or filling a cavity will eliminate your pain. If they are a good dentist, they do not just shove stuff in your mouth and tell you to trust them. Hopefully, they explain to you what they are doing and why it is going to help you. If you are convinced, you go through with it. Generally, if you are selling any product that does what it is supposed to do, you should not have many issues with the second part of the formula. This means that the crux of selling really hinges on the first part of the formula— establishing 'a pain' and a willingness on the customer's behalf to fix that pain. Quite simply, the second part of the formula does not exist without the first. You could convince someone that you sell the best burritos in town, but if they are not hungry, they probably are not going to eat a burrito. But even if you sell mediocre burritos, you will have an exponentially greater chance of selling to that same individual if they are hungry, because all you need to do is show them that you can satiate their hunger.

For that reason, I have always maintained that I would rather sell to a customer who is already using a competitor's product than a customer who is doing nothing at all. That is because you know that such a customer has already gotten past Part 1 of the selling process, which is understanding their pain. Not only does such a customer understand their pain, but they have been proactive enough to go out of their way to make the effort and the financial investment in fixing it. What remains in such a scenario is merely showing that customer that you have built a better mousetrap than the one they currently use. On the contrary, a customer who has no solution in place might not even be sold on the idea that they need a mousetrap. That means when you sit down with that customer, you have multiple inflection points in your selling process—one is identifying a problem that merits attention, and another is touting your solution as their best option.

This brings me back to the "yes" before the "yes." When establishing pain, I like to propose a hypothetical alternative scenario to the current state that involves my product and ask the customer if they would say "yes" to that situation. For example, if I were making plans with my colleague, Brendan, to see a movie, and Brendan was interested in getting something to eat instead, I might isolate his concern and ask him if he is otherwise interested in the movie in a vacuum. In other words, if his hunger were not a factor, would he be interested in seeing the movie? Once it is established that he does want to see the movie in a vacuum, the follow up question would be something like, "If I could show you a plan that involves getting food before the movie, would you be excited about seeing the movie?" Provided that he is satisfied by such a plan, the onus has been shifted from convincing Brendan that the movie is a good movie, and instead on whether or not I can deliver on a plan that includes both.

There is a famous example of a question often used in sales interviews where an interviewer asks the interviewee to sell them a pen. Interviewees make a pretty tragic mistake most of the time jumping right into how neat the pen is and how the individual must need something to write with. That is not how you establish pain. The way you establish pain is by understanding the individual: what do they do all day? Once you have that information, you can logically deduce which aspects of their life might require a pen. You then focus on those areas. When you have a good idea at work and you do not write it down, how much is that impacting the way you are recognized? When you are constantly staring at your phone because you have nothing to write with, how is that affecting your sleep? How would you quantify all that? And then the "yes" before the "yes,"—if this problem is costing you $10,000 in potential lost wages, would you be excited to spend $5 on a solution that I can have in your hand tomorrow? If the answer to that question is "yes" (and by this point, it absolutely should be), then the onus of the conversation has essentially been lifted. And that is because all you need to do at this point is show that you can deliver on this $5 solution called the pen that can be obtained through next-day delivery on Amazon.com. This last proposition—that you can provide a pen—is very easy to deliver on. But it is meaningless until the customer first establishes that they want one.

What I mentioned just now is a phenomenon of isolating the concern. This is nothing new for most seasoned salespeople, but I still want to discuss it briefly. I used to tell people who worked for me that customers do two things: they lie and they drag their feet. Now, at first glance, it might seem like I have an embittered attitude towards the people who I sell to, and that is not the case at all. The reality is, your customers are human beings just like you. That means they are emotional creatures. And emotional creatures have a hard time rejecting other people because it makes them feel bad. In this way, you can actually start to see your prospects as well-intentioned people when they are not completely truthful or drag their feet, even though your visceral reaction may be the opposite. Ultimately, this means that customers might have a propensity to be somewhat dishonest so as not to let you down, or that they might just drag their feet on giving you an answer simply because they do not want to say "no."

But because rejection is so difficult, we should actually admire people for having the courage to reject others. I remember in college it was my friend Eddie who came to tell me that I was not accepted into the social club I wanted to belong to. I have to imagine that he dreaded having that conversation with me, and hopefully I made it a little easier for him by keeping my emotions in check when he did. Yet in all the years since then, I have always remembered the sincerity with which he issued the news to me, and I always felt like he was equally disappointed to be sharing it with me, as he had little to no control over it. For that reason, there is a special kind of respect I have always had for him. And so not only should we embrace rejection when we get it, but we should also respect those who have the courage to be honest when they reject us.

Now, of course, in all of this, my philosophy is that I would rather get a "no" than a "maybe" for two reasons: First and foremost, at least with a "no" you understand that you need to move on. Now you are no longer wasting your time talking to a customer who is not ready for your solution, and you are no longer wasting their time either. Second, with a "no" you are much more likely to get a reason for why someone is not interested. And at least then you can attempt to overcome their objection. When you are stuck in MaybeLand (as I like to call it), there is a lot more hemming and hawing and much less direct dialogue about what concerns need to be rectified.

For that reason, you actually want to invite customers to say "no" to you if you can. Read that again because I know it sounds counter-intuitive. Do not be afraid of "no." Embrace it. After all, it is where the sale really begins. When I reach out to customers in my cold outreach or in a follow up after a prospect has gone cold, I will actually say something to the effect of, "It's OK if you are no longer interested," or even, "I prefer that you tell me that you are no longer interested if that is the case." By inviting a customer to say "no," you show them you are not there to be pushy. This disarms customers and makes them much more likely to be honest with you about how they are feeling.

In the absence of certainty of what a customer is really feeling, unfortunately you are left needing to ask questions and determining for yourself whether there is intellectual honesty in the responses that you are getting. When a customer tells me my product is too expensive for them, I isolate their concern by asking "Is that your only concern?" If the answer is "yes," I at least know now that this is the only obstacle I need to overcome. If the answer is "no," I welcome the laundry list of other reasons as well. Let's get all the cards out on the table. If we cannot do that, we will never overcome the objections because we will not know what they are. If the customer says that pricing is their only concern, my follow up question is simple: "If the product were free, would you go ahead with it right now?" This is not a real question. It is a test. What you are testing with this question is whether or not the prospect was truthful in their last answer. After all, if pricing is the only concern, the prospect should be prepared to say "yes" to a free product, because you have now eliminated the only obstacle. If the customer says "no" to this question, you now know that they were not being completely honest to you previously, and now you have an opportunity to extract the information you are really looking for. "What other concerns do you have then?" is what should come out of your mouth next, or, more plainly, "You just told me pricing was the only concern, but when I asked you about using it for free, you rejected my offer. Why is that?" This may seem confrontational, but you have earned the right to ask that question because honesty is a basic foundational principle upon which all dialogue should occur.

Now of course, getting to "yes" before the "yes" is ideal but not always possible. There could be a myriad of reasons why. For one thing, a customer might genuinely have a hard time understanding their pain or whether their pain is significant enough that they want to devote time and money towards a solution. Or the customer might just be a difficult person who wants to make your life challenging. Or, they might even be on board with acknowledgement of their pain, but unconvinced that you have a solution that solves for their pain. Just because it is easier to handle the second part of the sale—showing that you can deliver—does not mean that it is a slam dunk. Customers will have objections about all sorts of things, and your ability to follow through on your promises is within bounds for them to question. In other words, even if your customer acknowledges their own pain and you only need to show that you can solve their problems for them, you may very well still face objections about your ability to do so.

A natural instinct when it comes to handling objections is to tell the customer why they are wrong. I often hear the word "but" used. If you are overcoming an objection and you feel yourself starting to say the word "but," tape your mouth shut and re-read Chapter 4 about Inception. People do not like being made to feel stupid and they like ideas more when the ideas are their own ideas. So save your "buts" for someone else. Instead, embrace the word "and." The word "and" takes whatever your customer's reality looks like to them and then it includes you in that world. If I am selling a pen to someone and they tell me that the timing is not good right now because they already have some pens, you might reply by saying something like, "It sounds to me like you really value your pens, and that is why I want to make sure that you have some variety in what you are using."

As a general tenet and in keeping with my philosophy about authenticity, I would encourage you to consider asking open-ended questions when you are confronted with an objection. When in doubt, just ask yourself what you would do with your best friend or a family member. If your best friend had a boyfriend that you did not like, and your best friend came to you with an issue about said boyfriend, hopefully you would listen to them and try to be objective rather than imposing your agenda on your friend. This consists of gathering information. You might propose a solution that your friend rejects. The instinct might be to argue, but if you are a good friend, you would ask them why they reject your idea, and what alternatives they have. You might even run through those alternatives and see how they stack up against your idea. If your idea is the best idea, you will probably mutually come to that conclusion through inception—showing rather than telling. And that is far more powerful than the alternative where you impose your own personal feelings on your friend.

Let's say a prospect tells you that the timing is not good right now. You might ask why that is and you might ask if it is their only concern as a starting point. As we discussed before, you ought to isolate the concern before advancing much further, lest you leave any unvocalized concerns in your trail. But once you have done these things and you have an understanding of why the timing is not good, you should probably ask "when" is the right time. And then you should ask "What are you going to be doing between now and then?" These are all open-ended questions that give you a fuller picture of what is really going on. What I have found to be the case is that people are more or less all trying to solve the same types of problems—they want to be better, faster, more efficient. Whatever it is that a prospect might be electing to do instead of buying your product more likely than not is solving for a similar pain. They just might be labeling it as something else. For example, if you sell girl scout cookies door to door and someone tells you that the timing is not great right now because they are constantly at work, it is likely they are working so hard so that they can put food on the table for their family. And girl scout cookies are food. Their perception that the timing is not right is predicated on the very reason why they should be buying the cookies—you just need to work together to help them see that.

What you do then by asking these open-ended questions is arm yourself with knowledge to understand if you should be re-focusing your pitch. Perhaps you spent all this time pitching about how your tool works, when in reality, what you needed to be doing all along is show the prospect that it works better, faster, and less expensively than the other thing they think they need to be doing more urgently. After all, whatever that thing is, it is creating this objection about timing. You cannot get yourself this knowledge on what you need to do unless you ask the questions.

Long story short, when you ask such open-ended questions, what you tend to establish almost always is that the customer acknowledges their pain but has either prioritized a different pain or they have prioritized a different solution to their pain. Either way, you have established the first and most important part of your selling process, which is that pain exists. There is no way for you to overcome the objections you face unless you truly understand what they are. This necessitates asking many questions and continuously isolating concerns to make sure that you are getting the truth about what the concerns really are. Only when you truly understand what concerns exist can you start to tackle them. If it is an issue of prioritization, dig into why that is and try to quantify this specific pain versus other pains they are experiencing. If they believe a competitor offers a better solution, ask questions to understand why that is and continue to try to get "yes" before "yes!". Something as simple as, "If I could show you that we can do X, Y, and Z like our competitor, would you feel differently?" Be direct and ask questions. Treat the customer like a friend—someone who you respect for telling you "no"—and you will naturally be unafraid of asking questions that you thought would get you to "no," which ultimately can help you get to "yes."

Chapter 8

Take "Yes" For an Answer, Shut Up, and Be Concise

Every time you open your mouth to speak, you are increasing the odds that someone is going to take issue with what you have to say. That may sound like an ominous statement, but it is true.

I mean, think about it. If you say nothing at all, what can some-one possibly take issue with?

As you're reading this, you might be wondering if you are better off acting like a mime moving forward. I am not suggest-ing that you take a vow of silence for the rest of your life. What I am suggesting is that you stop believing that just because you feel compelled to say something, that it means it must be a good idea. Some of us have no filter whatsoever, and even for those of us that do have a filter, we have already acknowledged in previous chapters the flaws in our own thinking and our predisposition to say things that might offend others without even knowing it.

If you ever watch the show *Shark Tank* (and assuredly, you probably have, because there are hundreds of episodes and it is constantly on television), you will notice that most of the people doing the pitches are somewhat amateur-ish in their presenta-tions. This is actually what makes the show so enjoyable to so many people: it feels accessible. When everyday people like you and me get on the big stage to pitch products to tech and real estate billionaires, it makes us feel empowered like we could go and do that too. And while this is mostly a good thing, I do feel bad that some of the contestants on the show surely never received any sales training. One of the reasons I know that is because they rarely ever take "yes" for an answer.

What does it mean to take "yes" for an answer?

Taking "yes" for an answer means that when someone says "yes," you shut up. Mentally tape your mouth shut whenever you find yourself in this scenario. When someone gets to "yes," you have done your job. If you were having an argument with your significant other about something you wanted to do but one of you had to take care of the children, you would not ramble off all the reasons why it was a good idea for your partner to say "yes" after they have already said "yes" to you. For one thing, it might make them re-think their decision. But more importantly, you might actually end up saying something that they had not considered problematic before. As you start rambling about why you are so happy that you got your way, you might mention that now you will have an opportunity to hang out with a friend you have not seen in a while. Maybe it is the same friend that your significant other hates. See what you just did? Now you're sitting at home taking care of the kids because you could not just shut up and take "yes" for an answer.

In the sales setting, I actually see this manifest itself in very small, subtle ways. For example, I often hear sales reps saying "yeah" or "yes" in response to customers who are saying positive things while the customer is still talking, signaling that they are going to try to interrupt the conversation. If your prospect (or anyone for that matter) is giving you good energy, just sit there and let them give you good energy. There is no work to be done when people are already agreeing with you. If people feel like you are just itching to interrupt them to make them feel even smarter about their decision, it gives a weird, 'sales-y' vibe. Just sit there and be quiet and let the person tell you how excited they are. When they are finished, all you need to do is ask about next steps. You do not need to act as an echo chamber for the decision that they already seem to have made.

The expression that is most often used to describe this phenomenon is "talking past the close." I like "taking yes for an answer" because it sounds funnier. But just remember: once you have gotten to yes, it can only go downhill from there. The less you do from that point forward, the more you will get. The more you actually try to do, the higher the likelihood that you will unintentionally introduce a concern or some type of friction. What do I mean by "shut up?" This applies to the entire selling process, not just when you get a favorable response. Whenever I hear sales reps itching to butt into a conversation with a customer, I cringe. No one likes feeling like they are on the verge of being interrupted. Most salespeople know already that it is better when the customer is doing more of the talking. Why? Well, I just told you why. Think of the words coming out of your mouth as a poison. With enough of this poison, there is no antidote to cure the customer of the ills you have just inflicted upon them. By talking so much, by default it must mean that you are doing more telling than showing and not very much inception or understanding or listening. But also by talking you are unknowingly continuing to introduce more and more obstacles into your selling process. When a customer asks you about pricing and you give them your pricing and then mention that your pricing is better than your competitor's pricing, you have just made a fascinatingly common mistake. Not only have you gone out of your way to answer a question that was not asked, but in doing so, you have now introduced the existence of a competitor of which your customer may have been previously unaware. Good job—maybe you should start moonlighting for your competitor, bringing up their name every time someone does not ask.

This cuts nicely to the need for being concise. The more ideas you introduce to someone, the more complexity that is involved. The more complexity that is involved, the more likely it will be that there is something within that complexity with which others may disagree. Think about this in the context of what you experience in your life. If you were thinking of joining a club, and the club's mission was to do this one thing you were passionate about, you would probably be excited about it. But then if you found out that the club also cared about all these other things you disagree with, you would probably decide not to sign up, even though you still agree with them about other aspects of their mission. Complicating the mission statement makes it less appealing.

Think about the ads that are successful. NIKE's slogan is "Just Do It." It isn't some long-winded explanation about the price and quality of their shoes. It's a very simple idea. You know it when you see it. Apple's slogan is "Think different." When you think of Apple, you think of innovation. These are some of the most successful companies on the planet. They got there because they deliver a concise value proposition. The more and more they ramble on about why they do what they do, the more likely it is that you would find something that you do not like about it.

In the interest of following my own advice, I am going to let this be the shortest chapter in the book and end it here.

Chapter 9

The Customer is Not Always Right

I worked as a waiter for a local restaurant for parts of high school and college. There were many times when customers were rude to me for no apparent reason or did not tip me as much as they should have. I had to deal with a lot of screaming children and messes since it was a family restaurant. Of course, for every customer who did not live up to my expectations, there were several who were completely fine or who went above and beyond to make sure that I was recognized for my service. That experience taught me to really appreciate people who work in service jobs and to give them the benefit of the doubt even when it might be difficult, so I make sure to tip generously whenever I can. And yet somehow I had internalized back then to keep my mouth shut to all of the unruly customers who so blatantly disrespected me. Why is that?

There is a famous saying in the sales world: "The customer is always right." The phrase actually originated within the service industry and was created to help businesses have a mindset towards customer satisfaction. What is often intended with this phrase is that you sometimes need to swallow your pride when dealing with a customer and treat them like gold no matter what they do. If a customer gives certain feedback—even if the feedback is patently wrong—then you act as if the customer is right and you do something to make the customer feel like their voice is heard. This is complete and utter nonsense.

In 2017, a man named David Dao was dragged (literally) off of an oversold United Airlines flight after refusing to deboard the plane. When people saw the video, they were outraged, and many vowed never to fly with the airline ever again. I actually wrote an email to the CEO about his response to the incident, which I found to be problematic at the time (and he did not respond). To be sure, if you only watched the video and you knew nothing else, you would assume that United Airlines was barbaric in its treatment of this innocent customer. After all, it was their problem that the flight was oversold to begin with!

But when you peel the onion on that story, it actually starts to feel like United Airlines was the real victim. For one thing, the issue the airline had was that it needed to accommodate four crew members for the trip to Louisville so they could be present for a route that was leaving from that airport. While it was still the airline's fault, this was not nearly as bad as overbooking the flight. Further, the three other passengers who were selected at random to deboard the plane all left without a qualm. All four passengers were offered $800 vouchers, meals, hotels, transportation, and a ticket for a flight the next day. Technically, all four passengers had agreed to such an outcome in the terms and conditions of the tickets they had bought. David Dao seemed to be acting belligerently, it turned out, and he had allegedly had some serious skeletons in his closet, which the reader can look up and form their own opinion on. When you started to insert these other facts about the situation, the scales start to tilt: maybe it was the customer who shared in some of the blame for the situation, and the airline—always ripe for consumer criticism, it seems—that was inevitably going to bear the brunt of criticism.

Even though the viral video of David Dao being dragged off a plane ultimately served as negative press for the airline, I would argue that the sensation of viral videos in general has helped brands in their efforts to show that the customer is not always right. Before the age of viral videos, a customer could act as unruly as they wanted, and ultimately it would be the customer's word versus the brand's word as to what had transpired. But in today's day and age, people are all too keen to turn on their smartphone the moment they see someone acting unruly in a Walmart. How satisfying is it to watch someone mouthing off to a Starbucks barista about their right to not wear a mask during a global pandemic and see the person get thrown out of the venue? There was even a name coined for these types of people this past year. You are now called a "Karen" if you are a rude, entitled customer who talks down to people and asks to speak to the manager. It is engrained in our culture even that we should not accept petulant and childish behavior, and that we should in fact stand up to such behavior no matter the perceived hierarchy of those involved.

When you deal with someone in your personal life and you have an issue with something they say or do, you should feel comfortable enough to stand up for yourself and explain why you were hurt by that word or deed. Generally it is best not to point fingers but to merely explain how someone's actions made you feel and why, leaving them an opportunity to explain themselves and to apologize, if need be. This is what people do when they have respect for one another. If there is some lingering issue between me and my best friend, I trust him enough to remain friends with me if I bring up the issue to talk it out with him. It would actually be disrespectful not to, and it would be a sure indication that you might not have as much trust built as you thought previously.

When my best friend moved in with the woman who is now his wife after dating her for one month, I explained to him that I was worried about him moving too quickly. Mind you, I really liked his girlfriend because she is a great person and a great match for him, and she brings the best qualities out of my friend. I just did not want him to get hurt, especially since he had very little relationship experience at the time. I was very nervous about having that conversation with him because I knew there was a non-zero chance that he might interpret my motivations differently and subsequently choose his girlfriend over me. But I said what I had to say anyway because ultimately I cared more about his well-being than my own selfish interests. Fortunately, he understood. And actually, he thanked me for having the courage to say something to him that maybe his other friends were too timid to say. He told me that it meant a lot to him (even though he disagreed with me) because it showed him how much I cared about him. I think we both left that conversation feeling good about the outcome and knowing that we could always have difficult conversations with one another. In the end, he is happily married to a fantastic woman and we remain best friends.

If you kowtow to your customer's every need or behavior no matter how ridiculous or insulting it is, you are losing the opportunity to build the types of bonds you develop with close friends. Not only that, but you are ultimately signaling consciously or sometimes subconsciously that you are not being authentic in your relationship and that you really only care about collecting money from that individual. If I never had conflict with my best friend, he would probably start to wonder if I have any backbone. Conflict is normal and natural. It is how you respond to conflict that defines you and it is certainly what defines the best friendships and relationships as well. Lastly, not standing up for yourself certainly means that you will end up being unhappy. And in any relationship, it is important for both people to be happy.

If we have established that standing up for yourself and having difficult conversations are signs of respect, then why would anyone ever do the opposite in a sales setting? It is oft-forgotten that salespeople are exactly that: people. We have lives to lead and mouths to feed just like anyone else. Our interests matter just as much as the interests of our customers. The relationship between salesperson and customer is symbiotic: the customer pays the salesperson, and the salesperson delivers some type of value in return. It is not just the monetary and service aspects of the relationship that need to be equal. It is also the emotional aspect of the relationship that needs to be equal. The customer is not, by design, in the driver's seat, ordering around the sales rep. What do I mean by this?

Let's think about a scenario where you have spent a lot of time with a prospect but then they seemingly "go dark" for a period of time and they stop responding to your calls and emails. In the real world, this would be pretty rude. It is actually a fairly common phenomenon in the dating world these days for people to "ghost" one another. This is when you go on a date or a series of dates with an individual and then stop responding to any of their messages, disappearing like a ghost.

The way you respond to a customer who ghosts you is the same way you would respond to someone who ghosts you after a great date: you remind them that you have put a lot on the line in the relationship, that you find the behavior hurtful, and that you are wondering whether or not they are still focused on the initiative. If I was a few months deep into conversations with a prospect and they "ghosted" me for a month, of course I would consider some possibilities that have nothing to do with disrespect for my time. Maybe they got pulled in a different direction. Maybe they got sick. Maybe they are working on getting internal buy-in and trying to only get back to me once they have a meaningful update. That is why it is important not to point fingers and try to assume the best. But you still have to stand up for yourself. I would tell the prospect that I spent a lot of time working on the material we have been going over, their behavior seems uncharacteristic of our past dialogue, and I would ask point blank whether or not they are interested in continuing the conversation. This type of direct, somewhat confrontational communication almost requires a response—again, as long as it goes only that far and not to the point of insinuating any sort of bad faith on behalf of the prospect.

I recently had a prospect who kept rescheduling meetings with me right before we were scheduled to meet. Of course, I found this frustrating because my days are pretty tight schedule-wise and I had continuously blocked out times on my calendar that I could have spent talking to other customers. So that is exactly what I told this prospect. I said to him that I know he is really busy, but I am really busy too and that continuously moving our time around was affecting my ability to have conversations with other like-minded customers. I never accused the client of doing any of this purposefully or with ill-will. All I asked was a simple yes or no question: "Do you still want to get together, or is this not a high priority right now?" This goes back to what we discussed about Cold Outreach where giving the customer an "out" actually serves to show them your humanity and honesty, ultimately working in your favor. What ended up happening was that the prospect apologized to me, rescheduled the meeting for the last time, got on the phone with me, started the conversation by emphasizing how busy he was and how he did not mean to jerk me around, and then proceeded to go through the sales pitch with me.

In the interest of being fair, I need to emphasize how important it is not to try to embarrass people or undermine them. I had this approach backfire on me once when I was not as careful as I should have been. One time, my company had spent about a year working with a potential customer towards a proof-of-concept. The proof-of-concept was unceremoniously killed out of nowhere by the leader of the organization. We had had no communication with this individual previously and he seemed pretty far removed from all of the work that had been done between his team and ours. My internal champion there was very distraught, so I asked him if it would be helpful for me to write a firm but not antagonistic message to his business leader, and he agreed that that could be a good approach.

I made some key mistakes in my outreach. First and foremost, I did not write directly to the business leader, instead copying the entire team of decision-makers. This was a problem because no matter how softly I tried to position my message, there was going to be a chance that I embarrassed the business leader by allowing other people to see my message. That had the potential to alienate the recipient of my message. Second and more importantly, there were undertones to my message that subtly implied that the business leader was inconsiderate and not knowledgeable about our space. I say they were subtle because they were. I had known that they had evaluated a competitor of ours in the past, and I said something to the effect of "there are other options now," which implied that he did not understand the landscape of our space. Long story short, the message was not well-received. The prospect called me angrily and asked that I remove myself from working with them on that account moving forward. This is the only time such a thing has ever happened to me in my sales career, and I was embarrassed about it. He refused my attempts to extend the olive branch and he even sent a gift back to me that I tried to send as an apology. Long story short, do not infantilize people when you stand up for yourself, even if you are doing it implicitly.

Here is what I should have done.

What I should have done was set up a phone call, because talking things through is a lot easier than having a dialogue via e-mail. This is true of all things. How many times have you argued with someone via text message but then found that it was easy to resolve your issues in person or over the phone? How many times have you seen people yell at each other on Facebook who are otherwise compatible friends in real life? How many times have you been turned off by an e-mail because you read a certain tone in it? The issue with e-mail over direct dialogue is, of course, that the written word is rife with misinterpretation. People can inject their own meaning into what you are saying or they can inject a certain tone that you did not intend. In verbal expression, you can hear tone and intent much more clearly, and if you are face-to-face, that is even better because you can read body language.

Now, if you are not satisfied by that answer and want to know what a better written message would be, that is fine. If a phone call were not possible, a better message would have been direct to the decision-maker. This way, it would not feel like I was putting him on the spot. A better message would have been less verbose. A better message would seek to understand while re-affirming the time and effort of the many people who had been involved up to that point. I wish I might have said something like this:

"Dear Potential Customer,

I have been working with your colleague for the last few years on this project. We have devoted many hours of our team's time and your team's time working towards a proof-of-concept. Everyone has been really excited about this work because the business case we provided is very compelling (see attached).

I just learned today that you are no longer interested in pursuing this proof-of-concept. This has left many people on both teams feeling a little bit deflated after all the work we have done. Since I am in the dark on the motivations behind this, I thought I would reach out to you to seek to understand. Ideally, we can hop on a phone call so we can talk through what our options are, but in the absence of that, your insight on the concerns you might currently have is greatly appreciated.

Sincerely,

Frustrated Jeff"

This would have been a much better approach because it is a polite way of standing up for yourself. You are reminding the person that many people have spent time and effort on this project, and that they ought to appreciate the magnitude of the business case before nixing the project. Moreover, the most charged term in the e-mail is that people are feeling "deflated."

This is not a finger-pointing expression. This is a reality about how people are feeling. What would be bad is saying that people feel "cheated." Being cheated implies that the recipient of your message has cheated other people. That is accusatory. Whether or not someone has done something wrong, it is completely within reason to let them know how their actions have made you feel. There have been many times where I have been disappointed in the actions of other people and told them as much. More often than not, what this does is allow them to clarify their intentions in a way where I no longer feel disappointed. However, if I went into those conversations telling people "you screwed me over," chances are they would just turn off immediately and not even get to a point of wanting to make me feel better, because I just levied heavy charges against them without any effort to understand their motivations.

There is a difference between being helpful and being deferential. If your best friend was constantly failing in life, you would not kill them with kindness and act deferential to them. You would not tell them to just keep making the same mistakes. If they needed to be confronted with a harsh truth, you would give it to them if that was what was best for them to hear from you. Why should you treat your customers any differently? Stand up for yourself. Ironically, you are treating your customers with more respect by giving them the harsh truths they need to hear. You are not helping them by coddling them. Do not be afraid to do what is needed to help them succeed.

Chapter 10

Failure is OK.
Being a Victim is Not.

I came into the sport of wrestling by mistake. I had always played basketball for a winter sport growing up, and I had aspirations to make the basketball team when I started going to private school in 7th grade. If New England as a region is known for producing athletes in any sport, it is certain that hockey and basketball are amongst them. This leaves wrestling as the region's ugly stepchild as far as winter sports go—reserved for the worst of the athletes who were not good enough to make their respective hockey or basketball teams.

I was one of those unfortunate people. I remember how disappointed I was to see the cuts on the bulletin board and the revelation that I now had to find something else to do with my time. It all seemed very unfair to me at the time, and since I did not know how to skate, it left wrestling as my only option for a new hobby to take up that season. I did not even know that wrestling existed until then, and frankly, I wasn't very excited about it. After all, it was only the unathletic losers who were forced to do wrestling, or so I thought.

I spent most of my time in wrestling practices being confused about what was going on and just trying to make it through the season. My first ever match was at Providence Country Day. I walked out to the mat, not really sure if I had retained any of the moves in my head, just hoping for the best or that I would not embarrass myself. I thumped my opponent (somehow), realizing for the first time that maybe this wrestling stuff was not so bad after all. I ended up going 11-1 that season, my only loss coming in the finals of a tournament to a much more experienced opponent. Before the season had started, I was a middle of the pack athlete in gym class fitness testing. Once the season was over, I had the fastest 50-yard dash, I could do the most pushups, and I could jump further than anyone else in my class. In light of all of this, I decided to dedicate myself to being good at wrestling.

It was the first time that I felt like I was in control of my own destiny, and I liked winning.

Within the confines of New England prep wrestling, I had a relatively good career. I started on Varsity for four seasons and was elected co-Captain my senior year. I spent most of that season ranked #2 in all of New England, and after an unfortunate late season injury, I slid to what for me was a disappointing 6th place finish and a performance at the national tournament that did not meet my own expectations. Still, this was a relatively good career for where I came from. I was never close to being the best, and along the way, I was forced to come to grips with those shortcomings to push myself harder and harder. I never gave up while all at once forgiving myself for being human.

Phone calls started coming in from college coaches as my career was ending. These were mostly from small, local Division 3 schools I was not interested in going to anyway. A couple were interesting, including Williams College, which was very much on my list. I ended up doing a recruiting visit there and enjoyed it. But coming from a very competitive academic environment, my foremost priority was just to find the college I wanted to go to and try to get in there. If that school had a wrestling program and would let me continue wrestling, even better.

When I showed up at Princeton to do a college tour, I called the coach out of the blue and asked him if I could come and introduce myself. I walked down to his office and did just that. He had no idea who I was because I was not even remotely on his radar, and rightfully so. New England high school wrestling is not particularly renowned in the grand scheme of things as compared to other places, and moreover, I was not a regional star.

I said I was a hard worker and wanted to learn as much as possible, which was true. And the coach was very nice to me, encouraged me to apply to the university, and said he would be happy to let me practice with the team if I got in on my own merits.

I was very fortunate to find out months later that I was accepted into Princeton. The wrestling program underwent some change immediately thereafter, bringing in a new coach in an attempt to revive the program. A decade prior, the program had been disbanded due to Title IX, but the alumni organization swiftly stepped in to provide the funds to bring it back. In my freshman class, only one other wrestler was a true recruit. The idea was that the new coach would step up the recruiting with the university's cooperation and bring a new mentality to a program that had been the doormat of the Ivies for a little while. He has done exactly that, but we'll get to that later.

As freshman year began, so did my college wrestling career. Within two weeks of training, the one recruit in our class quit the team. He was roughly my size, so this immediately thrust me into the starting lineup. My plan when joining the team was just to work hard and maybe be good enough by my senior year to help the team. Those plans changed right away. Since this was a Division 1 program, I knew I was in for some major adversity.

Strictly from a training perspective, every part of my college wrestling experience was a wake-up call. In a nutshell, it was several orders of magnitude more difficult. In some ways, I started to resent my high school coach and teammates for not pushing me harder. Obviously, those feelings were unfounded, but I immediately felt regret that I had not started the sport sooner, done more camps, and worked harder. I had always thought that I was very determined and a hard worker, but the effort in college was so much more demanding that it really just made me feel like a fraud.

Wrestling in college was the hardest thing I have ever done by far. Being disciplined about making weight, being disciplined about working out in a very deliberate fashion twice a day, and seeing little success was incredibly challenging for me. Our coach would say that Princeton wrestlers were the toughest in the country because of the demands they had from a wrestling standpoint while also dealing with the intense academic pressures of being a student at Princeton. I believed him back then and I still believe that today.

I ended up wrestling on the team for almost two seasons, and I never won a match. Some of my opponents were future Olympians, like Frank Molinaro of Penn State, and many of them were All-Americans. Succinctly, I was always punching out of my weight class. It was never easy, and it wore on me. But I was proud to be challenging myself. And even though I did not get the results that I wanted, it calloused my mind in a way that was life-changing. I learned more technique in those seasons than I did in all of the seasons I spent wrestling beforehand, and I still use many of them today when training Brazilian Jiu-Jitsu. As the great former wrestler and coach Dan Gable once said, "Once you've wrestled, everything else in life is easy." And that mantra has proven to be true for just about anything. When I am having a really tough workout, I always tell myself that it's not even close to as hard as what I did in college. When I am having a really tough day, I tell myself it's not as tough as those times. Nothing can stack up to how hard that was for me because as I already said, it was the hardest thing I have ever done by far.

Deciding to leave the team was a painful moment for me. The coach told me I would regret it, and I remember feeling at the time that that was funny because of how hard it was. And while it probably was the right decision for me at that time, it does not change the fact that I think about it almost every single day. It drives almost every single thing that I do. What I realized in that experience is that quitting at something does not sit well with me. Even if it is something incredibly difficult that 99.9% of people choose not to do—like wrestling for a D1 college program—if I start it, I want to finish it.

One of the best chapters of the book *Think and Grow Rich* is a story about the man who almost struck gold. As you can probably guess, it is about a gold miner who gives up on his job when he is one strike away from striking gold and changing his life forever. That resonated with me because when you are the man who almost struck gold, you have no way of realizing it. When I liken that to my own experience, it makes me wonder: how close was I to starting to realize the fruits of my labor, and how would that have impacted my decision and my life? When I was a teenager, I lacked a critical toughness because I had had no watershed moment of dealing with adversity. In retrospect, I was relatively fortunate and was not hardened as a result. Questioning myself and pushing myself for what seemed like every waking second of nearly two seasons was the greatest challenge for me at that time, and wondering "What if?" has made me realize that I never want to ask that question ever again. And in many ways, I did feel like a man who almost struck gold, because once I quit the team, we forfeited my weight in the team's next match to an opponent I had defeated three times in my senior year of high school.

That realization has set in for me in many facets of my everyday life. I was an early employee at a tech startup and things have not always been easy there. Especially in the early days when we faced a series of issues that never seemed to go away, and with other employers coming to me and promising me what they perceived to be much better opportunities, I must have thought about quitting at least 100 different times. And even in moments where it felt obvious to me and any objective observer that that was what I should do, I could never bring myself to do it. "What if," I asked myself, "I am the man who almost struck gold?" I did not want to have another moment of my life where I looked back with unanswered questions about what could have been or who I was. It turned out to be a good decision. I am having great success in my role, with autonomy and impact on the organization, and I get to work with the best and brightest people on the planet, several of whom are actually Princeton wrestlers. It goes without saying that I know firsthand what they are capable of and admire them for being able to finish a job that I could not.

The experience helped me to redefine what "failure" means. I don't regret giving it my all and not getting the result I wanted. I don't look at falling short as failure. I look at giving up as failure. Contextualizing things this way allows me to re-focus difficult times to give the extra push I need to reach the finish line. It's OK to not always be the best, as long as we are constantly giving our all and not giving in.

Whenever I think about giving up at anything large or

small—a work problem, a friendship or relationship challenge, an athletic endeavor—I think twice. Is the pain I am feeling now a temporary pain? How will I feel if I can overcome it, and how will I feel if I do not? Most importantly, how will I feel if I at least try to overcome it and fall short versus just giving up? I can't say that I am the best salesperson, the best grappler, or the best human being, but it sure feels a lot better knowing that I am trying my best at every single thing I do. What's more motivation is that Princeton now has one of the best teams in the country. The same coach took arguably the worst team in Division 1 wrestling, a group of students who just happened to want to try wrestling, and has entirely changed the culture to the polar opposite. Watching that from afar, it is hard to make excuses for myself any more. It certainly feels a lot better not to.

A relative to failure is accountability, and I want to talk a little bit about how accountability and failure go hand-in-hand with one another both within my life and in other real-world examples. When I quit the wrestling team, it took me a very long time to gain any sense of accountability for the decision. I made all sorts of excuses for myself and why it was OK. The most common excuse I made was that I was a walk-on, and so I never had a real commitment to anyone else to be doing something I did not want to do. Another excuse was that I had academic and extracurricular interests that were being put to the side as a result of the immense time commitment. Or that I just started the sport too late and that the amount of effort it was going to take to even be competitive simply outweighed how much I wanted it.

It's not that any of the above are bad reasons, necessarily, or that the decision was the wrong one. It's that they all ignored my own role in the events. Plain and simple, I wasn't tough enough to weather the storm during that time. That's a difficult thing to admit to yourself. When the easy thing to do is to walk away and blame others, the hardest thing to do is to keep going and attribute it to yourself. Where accountability intersects between those two outcomes is the acknowledgement that only you are responsible for what you do and what outcomes you obtain. And yes, even when external factors are weighing you down, you are always in control and capable of overcoming them—it just comes down to how badly you want to.

Take my coach for example. He inherited quite possibly the worst team in Division 1 wrestling. The level of commitment from members of the team was poor. We got blown out in all of our matches. He could have made excuses for himself—"there is not a commitment to recruiting" or "the talent level is not good enough" or "it's too hard to get good wrestlers into Princeton." But he knew what he was getting into when he took the job (although honestly, I bet he was still surprised). A decade later, the program is among the best in the country. That did not happen by mistake. That happens by accountability in bad times, when you do not look good but people trust you for your leadership and ownership, which in turn allows you to reap all of the rewards of success (e.g., people now know that success did not happen by mistake).

I remember one occasion which I wish I could take back. After a difficult practice, the coach told me I was not working hard enough. I was at my wit's end at this point and really felt like I was going above and beyond, so I stormed out of the room. I couldn't believe that in spite of my best efforts, it wasn't enough.

I just wasn't very good, I thought. The coach came to the locker room to find me and pulled me aside. He told me he wanted me to stick with it—surely, he knew I was at a breaking point. But the reality of his message did not sink in for me until years later, because in that moment I did not want to hold myself accountable to what he was saying.

This was the reality: the bar I had set for myself was very low. I wanted to be able to say that I was competent by the end of my career. That's not necessarily a low bar for the Average Joe who has never signed up for wrestling practice, but it was a low enough bar that it hurt me. One of the best concepts I utilize in my life today is Visualization—visualizing what I want all the time. The net-net is that I often end up pushing myself harder as a result of not being where I want to be at the right time. In college, I was expecting to lose every single time I set foot on the mat. I was not visualizing being a national champion, and naturally, my results suffered. But because I was not visualizing the highest level of success, my standard for what was an "above and beyond" effort was different than the athlete who actually had set that higher bar. This is the message my coach was trying to get me to understand. Back then, I did not want to hear it.

Being accountable is hard because sometimes it is a recognition of failure in some regard. No one likes being told they did something bad. But I liken lack of accountability to a Failure with a capital F: not only did you mess up, but you refused to understand your part in it, so surely you will never fix the mistake properly. And that's precisely the thing—being accountable is not failure, it is the opportunity to correct failure and to show others that you can correct failure. A valuable lesson I learned and one that seems to be missing in a lot of our dialogue today.

What I will say, however, is that we unfortunately live in a time where every one of us seems to have an opinion on the accountability of others. Whether it was a tweet from ten years ago, an offhand joke at the bar, or a viral video we see on the internet—we are all pretty quick to rush to judgment and become the arbiters of justice on who needs to be held accountable and to what degree. What seems to be lost in all of this is the willingness of the apparent wrongdoer to step forward and own up to whatever they did in the interest of moving forward. I prefer to live in a world where we care more about ownership and less on expecting human beings to not be human. Because the reality is, we are all humans, and therefore we are all ripe to miss the mark from time to time. What separates the wheat from the chaff is how we own up to it.

So what is the lesson here?

It's simple: with failure must come accountability. The accountable person owns their mistakes and corrects them. The unaccountable person blames others for their misfortunes and continues to fail. The accountable person is admired for being brave, the unaccountable person is ridiculed for being weak-minded. When we fail, it is easy to see how being accountable is the most productive path towards getting back on our feet.

There is a pretty important misconception to clarify about failure, and it has to do with our perceptions of failures. Realistically, it is not people who fail that others look down on. It is people who have no accountability for their failure and who make no attempt to rectify their past actions that we really do not like. People actually seem to admire failures, as long as they are working towards trying to be successful. We view it as human and we relate to that type of experience, because we all have our own failures, and we understand what someone else might be going through. In fact, we often celebrate the people who seem to overcome the odds. It is why people often cheer for the underdog in sporting events. Whether you like Tom Brady or not, most people respect him because he used to be a chubby 6th round draft pick with no real prospects of succeeding in the NFL, and he turned himself into perhaps the best player in the sport's history. His past failures as a college player or in his preparation for the NFL were of much less import than his current standing as someone who refused to accept mediocrity as his fate.

How does this relate to selling? You can probably already guess. There is a natural inclination in sales to feel that half of the outcome is out of your power because you cannot control what someone else will ultimately decide to do. This is a terrible inclination to have. As Mark Manson says in *The Subtle Art of Not Giving a F*ck,* there is a difference between fault and responsibility. It may not be your fault that a customer is being stubborn, but it is still your responsibility to fix their stubbornness. If you want to be successful in sales, you need to embrace failure and hold yourself accountable for your failures. If you avoid being wrong at all costs, you will never improve and you will never adapt to why people are saying "no" to you all the time. When you slip up in some affair concerning your family or your best friend, chances are you own up to it, say sorry, learn from it, move on, and do better next time. It should be no different in how you treat yourself in your sales career. You owe it to your co-workers and your customers to be growth-oriented and to hold yourself responsible for any failure even if it is not necessarily your fault.

This is, of course, very true in our current dialogue in politics. It seems as if nobody who is partisan these days is capable of ever admitting that their team—Team Red or Team Blue—has done anything wrong. To people on the far left and the far right, this seems perfectly acceptable and they apologize for nothing. The net result is that everyone else observes and forms a very different opinion. What ends up happening is that others look at what is going on and question the intellectual consistency of those who espouse such views. It feels hypocritical that those who claim to be so tolerant shout people down and throw heavy objects at them over political disagreement, or even support those who do; likewise, it feels hypocritical that those who call for civility in discourse seem to dance on the graves of their political opponents. The net effect is polarization.

Like I said before, it's really people who lack accountability that bother us, not people who fail all the time. People who fail all the time but hold themselves accountable by continuing to try to get back on their feet are actually quite admirable. We like those people and we want to help them because they are being realistic, honest, and motivated. People who just stubbornly refuse to admit that they ever do anything wrong or that there are some inconsistencies in their beliefs are just unpleasant to be around. This is why intellectual honesty is so crucial for our broken dialogue today. Whether you like it or not, nobody is going to take you seriously if you never take accountability. Even if you are the victim of circumstances beyond your control, you have two choices: you can complain, or you can do something about it. In today's on-demand social media driven culture, it is much easier to complain. This is why you see grievance as a religion.

This idea of accountability manifests itself in sales settings. There is a famous line in *Glengarry Glen Ross* where one of the salespeople decries, "The leads are weak!" He is blaming bad leads for his inability to perform his job function properly. Alec Baldwin's character—who I do not necessarily like, since he very negatively stereotypes the persona of a sales leader—retorts, "You're weak!" Though he is a little bit over the top in how dismissive he is to one of the sales reps, I agree with his message. It is a weak-minded individual who only blames their external circumstances and does nothing within their locus of control to alter their situation. I actually met with a member of my own team not long ago looking for feedback on how I could overcome a challenge pitching against a specific competitor. The issue felt like it was out of my control since I could not change the breadth of our functionality versus theirs. He shifted the onus back on me, suggesting that all sales problems are my problems since I am the sales leader in the organization. I ended up fundamentally re-shaping how I spoke about our product, which actually served to overcome the problem that I thought I had no control over. Customers liked this new version of the pitch and it has paid dividends. It was only by accepting that I had some agency in improving my situation that I was able to reach this conclusion.

There is actually a natural connection between accountability and authenticity. As I mentioned just a moment ago, people do not look down on people who fail, but they look down on people who lack accountability for their failure. When someone you know makes a mistake but owns up to it and apologizes, as long as you are a reasonable person, you probably appreciate their self-awareness and willingness to improve. But when someone wrongs you in some way and then refuses to take any ownership for their actions, you probably view that person in a different way. That is because based on all of the available information, they are not holding themselves to task on something. Therein lies the relationship between accountability and authenticity. Accountable people are authentic because being accountable requires a level of vulnerability that can be uncomfortable. No one likes to admit they screwed up. Doing so requires a level of honesty and introspection that is laudable for those who witness it. But when you shirk responsibility for your own actions, in a way you are shirking responsibility for being your authentic self. The authentic "you" deep down knows that you have done wrong, and that you are creating excuses to deflect responsibility and blame. The real "you" is hiding inside, huddled with your hands over your face as a fake "you" tells the lie that you are responsible for nothing, that your political stances have no flaws, or that it is other people who need to work on being less offended.

Approach your life and your sales career in the same way: anything that happens to you is your responsibility. Fix it. Anything that you do that creates your current situation, you need to hold yourself accountable for. Be accountable. You could be nothing but a failure your entire life but people will always respect you as long as you hold yourself accountable. The moment you start making yourself a victim of your circumstances is the day you stop growing.

Chapter 11

Hiring

In your real, everyday life, you consciously choose to surround yourself with a certain group of friends. What you care about in your friends tends to evolve over time. When you are younger, you might value attributes in others that you come to regret later in life. Many people are familiar with the movie *Mean Girls* starring Lindsay Lohan as geeky high-schooler Cady Heron. Cady becomes infatuated with a materialistic and cruel clique of girls because she thinks they will help her fit into her surroundings at a new high school. By becoming like them, she learns the hard way that this is not the type of person she truly wants to be. In the end, she apologizes for all of her misdeeds and returns back to her authentic self. She was ultimately much more well-liked by all of her peers in her more natural state of being. Wonder why that might be?

As we mature, we learn from the errors of our past and we start to see the value in lasting traits. Lasting friendships are built upon worthy traits: honesty, trust, care, empathy, and so on. When it comes to hiring at any company, why should it be any different? If you have the opportunity to choose a team to work with, you want the same types of traits in those people that you would expect out of close friends. This fosters goodwill amongst the team and sincere empathy in all situations. And let's face it, you would work a lot harder for a common goal when you are doing it with other people you respect and for whom you want the best possible outcomes than if you were working with people that you did not really care about at all.

As Alec Baldwin says in *Glenngarry Glen Ross*, sales is a tough racket. You need to have a thick skin, you need to be able to work hard, and you need to be a great listener and empathizer. I spent most of my childhood aspiring to be a professional athlete when I was older, and when it became pretty evident early on that that was not going to happen, I had to resort to a Plan B. But while most of my classmates in college had seemingly mapped this out from a young age—prepared to go into finance, consulting, medicine, or law—I was not so sure about what I wanted to do. I applied for teaching jobs, because I was interested in teaching and being a mentor. I applied for jobs in sports management, because I liked sports and had spent a summer interning with the Boston Red Sox. I applied (and was summarily rejected) to jobs in finance and consulting, because an English major does not get you very far in that arena.

Then I stumbled upon a job for a tech startup in Boston called SCVNGR. The CEO had dropped out of Princeton and gone to high school near me in Boston. The company was doing some very interesting things, and they had posted a sales position with high upside. I was very excited about this because I had always considered myself a hard worker, and I liked the idea that it was within my own hands to "write my own check" based on my work ethic. Some of my greatest flaws are my biggest strengths—namely a fear of failure and the everlasting anxiety and drive that accompanies that fear. I had always enjoyed public speaking and did not fear cold conversations. I applied for the job and I was hired. The rest is history—SCVNGR eventually changed its name to LevelUp and was acquired by Grubhub for $390 million, and I set the path for an enjoyable and successful sales career.

Over the years, I have interviewed for various sales positions and I have interviewed and hired people for various sales positions. I don't have a checklist and the questions I have asked have changed over the years, and what I look for is intrinsically different depending upon the role. But if there are some commonalities that have existed over the years, roles, and differing situations, I have ranked such traits below in order of their importance, ending with the most important.

5. Coachability

No one is perfect. And on top of that, every role and company are different, with different cultures, values, and ways to succeed. The best rep at Company A might look completely different than the best rep at Company B. Those reps might not succeed if they changed jobs based on their own strengths and what it takes to be successful in their respective roles. This means that anyone—including the sales leader—needs to be coachable.

Without coachability, you end up with stubborn people who believe it is "my way or the highway." They lack accountability and they cherish their ego greater than they cherish their own long-term success. A thick-skinned individual views coaching as a positive—it is a sign that their leader believes they have potential and wants to help them unlock it.

The simplest way to determine coachability is to ask someone about a time they reacted to negative feedback. I also like to give exercises throughout the interview process, render feedback to the individual, and see how they react to it. Do they defend their behavior or are they willing to give an inch? This will show you the willingness of the individual to accept and respond to feedback.

4. Accountability

Accountability is somewhat of an extension of coachability, because it is generally an accountable person who is open to being coached. An accountable person puts their ego aside in the short term for the benefit of their ego in the long-term. An accountable person recognizes that even when the customer seems to struggle to understand something, that the onus is on them for being unable to speak the customer's language. We are not here to just take orders—you can hire anyone to take an order. There should be an expectation that there will be friction and the right person—an accountable person—blames themself for failure to overcome that friction. They do not blame the customer, they do not blame the marketing team, and they do not blame the CEO or the product team.

I even encourage reps on my team to use accountable language when they are trying to overcome an objection. I teach people not to say "but" and then explain why someone is wrong. Instead, I encourage them to say something like, "I think it is a failure on my part to not have conveyed the information in a way that makes sense." By being accountable and accepting responsibility for not getting someone on board with an idea, it makes that other person feel like it is still up to them to come to your conclusions on their own. And we have already established that it is imperative that that be the case for people to end up agreeing with you.

Accountability is crucial because without accountability, there is never improvement. You just have the same person who loves taking orders and doesn't try to figure out why they are unable to take orders from the people who say "no." The best way to determine someone's accountability is to ask them directly about their failures and what they learned from them. Do they start pointing fingers? Or can they show moments where they slipped up, learned something, and then used it to succeed?

3. Honesty

My high school had a mantra that still sticks with me to this day: "Honesty is expected in all dealings." It was the first line of the school handbook. There was zero tolerance for lying and students were subject to suspension or expulsion for dishonesty.

It is important to hire honest people. You need honest people so that you can have honest internal dialogue about what is and is not working. Honesty is crucial for real coachability and account-ability. A dishonest person messes up key business indicators (the metrics used to measure performance), gets in their own way, and erodes trust throughout the entire organization.

More importantly, you need honest people because customers deserve honesty. Some of the best compliments I have been given are when customers tell me I was honest the whole time and interested in helping them, not trying to sell them something. It is easy to spot the difference. Even though I am a salesperson, I engage with salespeople all the time who sell me tools or tickets to trade shows. It is the honest people that I enjoy working with the most. I respect them for their honesty and for painting me a fuller picture. I can see through everyone else. You should expect the same of your client base when you hire in sales.

How to know if someone is honest? Ask them difficult

questions. I often find salespeople who, when pressed upon their greatest weakness, will make up some nonsense that is really a strength of theirs. I ask people what is their greatest fear about working for me or at my company. What is something that could make it go wrong? What has gone wrong in the past? How did they adjust? Challenge them. Anyone who pretends that their entire career is rainbows and butterflies is not being truthful and you should not hire them. If you want honesty in a candidate, you want to hear about their mistakes. So many interviews today are just both sides walking on eggshells asking canned questions and giving canned responses. If you want to find real people who truly suit your interests, make it uncomfortable and you will find out real fast who is authentic and who is not.

2. Listening

I was successful early in my sales career because I worked incredibly hard. It did not hurt that I was comfortable giving presentations and had a good communication and writing style. But I was not a good listener. I thought sales was all about making my point, giving my demo, showing everyone how "cool" the thing was that I was selling. Like I said—I ended up OK, but I often think about how much better I would have been if I had adopted a "listen first" attitude.

Sales is not about you. It is about the customer. If you treat the customer like your friend, you end up listening to the customer like you would listen to your friend. You end up asking them the questions you would ask your friend, not the questions you would ask someone to try to corner them into thinking you have a good product. All this to say, sales come naturally to those who actively listen with a keen, genuine interest in what the customer has to say. For that reason, it is important to hire salespeople who listen. I make sure of this not only in the steps along the interview process, but also to see how someone answers my questions. Are they answering the questions I am asking, or just giving me what I want to hear? Are they following up to understand why I am asking certain questions? Are they interviewing me, too?

1. Hunger

Listing this as #1 is not to take away from anything else on the list; of course, I always want honest, accountable, coachable listeners. But there is simply not a great salesperson on Earth who is not very hungry. I expect that someone has chosen a career in sales because they like being in control of their own destiny, because they believe in themselves and because they want to make the most of it. Some of the salespeople I have admired the most are very rough around the edges but have given an impression that they would hide a body for the job (N.B. to any lawyers reading this, that was a joke).

Simply put, salespeople require the utmost motivation to succeed. They need motivation to want to be coachable so they can be as good at their job as possible. They are accountable to themselves because they want to succeed and be better, not so they can hide and accept their failures. They do things the way they are supposed to be done because they are constantly bettering themselves and because that is the way they are wired. This is an irreplaceable, must-have trait for the best salespeople.

What else matters when you think about hiring? It's actually a topic we covered in the last chapter: intellectual consistency. It is important to always feel like people are treating one another fairly and that they are not beholden to selfish interests or an agenda that is not aligned with your principles.

Think about it: when you get angry about someone else's opinion, is it simply the opinion itself that upsets you, or is it that you find such an opinion to be intellectually inconsistent with other beliefs that the individual has? In my experience, intellectual inconsistency—a longer way of calling someone a hypocrite—is manifest in all of our unhealthy dialogue.

What angers us deep down is that we think people who disagree with us are hypocrites. When we find someone we disagree with, our instinct is to use some sort of analogy to show them that they are hypocrites. I'm guilty of this, too. I recently could not believe that there were people who staunchly opposed wearing masks in the midst of a pandemic. My reaction when dialoguing with such individuals is to ask them if they also oppose driving the speed limit, wearing a seatbelt, or even wearing clothes. After all, these are laws designed to protect people from themselves (and, especially in the case of clothes, to protect others). Such a retort is useful insofar as it might show someone the inconsistency in their thinking, but then again, when you call someone a hypocrite (even implicitly), you are unlikely to get very far. Because a hypocrite by definition will not admit they are a hypocrite even when they know they are a hypocrite. Say that three times fast. But think about it—it's true.

The people we tend to respect the most in difficult conversations are those who truly seem open-minded and who have some non-attachment to their own ideas. That is, they are willing to be wrong. What happens a lot of the time in my observation is that people who would otherwise have a more nuanced opinion about a certain issue will reject the nuance in favor of simplicity simply because they do not want to agree in the slightest with people they don't like or respect. If time after time you see people who generally disagree with you acting like hypocrites and never acknowledging fault, you inevitably will start to feel like you must disagree with those people no matter what, lest you end up on the wrong side of an issue.

This is a horrible way to approach things. And the reason I am writing this sidebar is because in hiring, it is incredibly important to find people who behave with intellectual honesty. Why? Because you and everyone on the team will take them more seriously, and so will your customers. We have already established that tension is abound when we sense intellectual dishonesty. It stands to reason that the inverse is true—that trust and respect are bred from those who think freely and clearly and without personal biases.

In a past role, an older and more respected sales rep poached leads out of my territory. The sales leadership in that company condoned his behavior because he was the top performing rep on the entire team and I was brand new. I found this disconcerting. When I raised the alarm on this to my manager, I was told to simmer down, and that I should be deferential to the other rep because of all the time and effort he had put into the company. This is textbook intellectual inconsistency: you cannot establish a set of rules for a team and then immediately be prepared to break them based on whoever your top performer is at any given time.

This fuels mistrust amongst everyone else on the team and makes it seem as though leadership is only concerned about themselves and not about all members of the organization. And this is one reason why people might leave a company.

One of my favorite comedies of all time is the movie *Cedar Rapids*. It is about an insurance salesman named Tim Lippe (played by Ed Helms, of *The Hangover* and *The Office* fame). Tim Lippe is from a small town in the Midwest and gets to go to his first ever sales conference, a regional event for midwestern insurance sales practitioners in Cedar Rapids, Iowa. I think I find the movie so endearing because it really touches on all the elements of sales conferences in general. I have gone to a lot of random cities throughout the United States and seeing Lippe's excitement about getting a bag of airline peanuts reminds me of the times early in my sales career when staying in a cheap hotel in another city seemed luxurious. Anyway, as the movie goes on, Lippe becomes aware that his company has been bribing the conference association's President for years to give them an annual recognition. For much of the film, he believes that this is his chance to prove himself to his higher-ups—to continue this trend of cheating and treachery. However, he has a "Come to God" moment at the end of the film when he tells everyone at the event what has been going on. He eventually leaves his company and takes the risk of starting his own venture with his existing clients, now feeling emboldened by the newfound maturity he has realized after his first ever adult work trip. Though exaggerated for Hollywood and comedic effect, this is a great example of intellectual honesty and doing the thing that is right to do even if it is not the thing that is most comfortable.

What is the takeaway? Practice what you preach. Be intellectually honest with those who you hire and expect the same in return. When you find people who cannot remove their own selfish interests and biases from helping the team grow, remove them. Your team will perform better if it is filled with people who are ready to help one another. Setting that type of culture starts with the leader: you.

Summarily, hiring should be no different than how you determine your best friends. The only real difference should be the context: in a work setting, you are looking for people with shared professional values. In a personal setting, you look for people with shared values, or people with whom you enjoy spending time. I try to avoid asking the canned interview questions and focus on the things that actually matter to me within the context of the work that I am doing. If what I value is work ethic, my interview is focused around determining who will have the strongest work ethic. If what I value is trust, I want to hear the candidate tell embarrassing stories about their past, because it shows they can be honest and laugh at themselves and from that I know I can trust them. Bring your authenticity to the process. At the end of the day, you are doing nobody any favors if both you and the candidate are both pretending to be people that you are not.

Chapter 12

The Real World

When I was younger, I used to be obsessed with the reality TV show *The Real World*. I think it was in large part because I was a kid and the lifestyle of an attractive twenty-something living in a big city with other attractive twenty-somethings appealed to me. I anticipated that what I saw depicted in the show was a reflection of real life. And yet, in real life, you really do not get locked in a co-ed mansion with a variety of people with serious personality disorders who are constantly at odds with one another while cameras follow their every move. As I got older, I went from feeling let down by this to feeling relieved by it. The lives these people were living were fake, and as fun as it might be to have no obligations and to party all the time, you start to realize that those people often become the most depressed of all. Why? Because they aren't being true to themselves.

This leads to a fundamental question that you might have had since you started this book: what if I am not a good person? Should I be my authentically lousy self? Surely, authenticity cannot be a winning strategy for everyone, because some peoples' personalities are much more desirable than others. Is this the "A-HA!" moment that sinks my hypothesis about successful selling, both in the real world and within the sales world?

Not quite. We need to divorce "good traits" from "authenticity." Good traits that I have discussed like honesty, empathy, work ethic, and others are not necessarily inherently present. Regardless of your personality though, people will always be able to tell whether or not you are acting with authenticity. And that will always matter, and yes, that includes if you are authentically a lousy person. Because if you are a lousy person, it is better to be authentically lousy than a fake lousy person. You might fool some people in the latter scenario, but it is hard to fool them all.

That being said, we should all strive to make ourselves authentically feel these traits. What I am trying to say is that no one is perfect and it is a noble and worthy goal to be the best people that we can be. I think part of that is first by being authentic. In being authentic, you will actually acknowledge your own shortcomings rather than pretend they do not exist. That in and of itself will attract people to you. In my experience, people are much more drawn to flawed people who admit their flaws and desire change for themselves than fake people who try to seem perfect. These flawed people resonate with us because we are keenly aware of our own flaws, and seeing others have the courage to be open about theirs makes us feel like we have something in common, whether or not we are ready to admit it.

Being a genuinely empathetic person is worth striving towards. You might find that when you try to practice this with a customer that you will feel you are not being authentic, because you are trying to adopt a behavior that does not feel natural to you. And that would be true. But there is a stark difference between feigning empathy for self-interest versus feigning empathy for altruistic reasons. Intention matters. And when your intention is that you want to be a better person for the world around you, I am hard-pressed to say that anyone should blame you for it. This is my long-winded way of saying that you should always be true to yourself, and that you should always understand that you still have more to learn. If you are not a different person ten years from now than you are today, you should question whether that is because the world around you is dry and boring, or whether it is because you are resistant to change.

A phenomenon you will see all the time whether you work in sales or not is the idea of "social selling." On a high level, this can mean a lot of different things: selling via networking, selling via referrals, selling via social media, and more. One of its most common manifestations is people putting out neutral content to their friends or followers. I use the term "neutral" because most often than not, they are not overtly selling themselves or their products. Of course not—we established in Chapter 1 that people are turned off when they sense they are being sold to. These "social sellers" often use a platform like LinkedIn to post content to position themselves as thought leaders who can be trusted.

I am all for this, as long as you mean what you say. And unfortunately, many of the people who engage in this practice very clearly are adhering to a schedule of posting simply for the sake of posting (and therefore, for the sake of selling). It is not for the sake of authentically feeling a need to share something. Ask yourself how many times you have seen a dramatic LinkedIn post that has the same number of sentences as it does paragraphs, like this:

When I was younger, I did not have much.

I did not get down on myself.

I worked really hard.

My hard work paid off, and I got into a great college.

I faced more adversity, and now I am super awesome.

This is why you read my posts on LinkedIn.

Does anyone talk like that in real life? Or just Presidential candidates when they stare into the teleprompter to tell you to vote for them?

I decided to take a vastly different approach. I focus on what I am thinking and feeling and how I can actually provide value. Since I work in the fraud space, I once posted about a fraud scheme my elderly grandmother was succumbing to in genuine search of help and I was overwhelmed with replies from people within my network who were there to help me out. Some of them networked with one another and a couple of them took an interest in me and my business, even though I was not soliciting their business. Sometimes, I just post short stories I have written in the past, because maybe people might enjoy reading them. Is that weird? Maybe. Is it authentic? Yes. I once had a customer tell me over dinner that one of the reasons they really enjoyed working with me was because I put great, authentic content out on LinkedIn. It was actually the last thing I was expecting to hear, but it warmed my heart, and it warmed my heart precisely because I knew that this was really a reflection on me. After all, I had not been acting when I put these things out there.

Embrace your authenticity in all that you do, especially when you are overtly selling yourself. When I sit down for any sort of interview for a job or a volunteer opportunity and people ask me what makes me tick, I do not make up some phony motivational story. I tell the truth. I grew up with a kind of neurotic Jewish mother who pushed me really hard in everything that I did. I am on time for every meeting, I never miss a deadline, and I out-work everyone else because my mother instilled that in me. I talk about it in a positive and light-hearted way, that I have all this anxiety about success because of my stereotypical over-anxious Jewish mother. And that is because it is entirely true. Without my mom's support, guidance, and motivation, I would not be any-where close to where I am today. Interviewers see that for what it is—that I must be telling the truth because it is so unabashedly personal. This makes them actually believe what I am saying; it shows them that I am honest and direct, and most importantly, it gives them faith I really will not lose.

As the interview goes on, I will talk about how this childhood of trying to earn good grades and play competitive sports every season affected me in my adult life. I tell the story about my first sales job and how when we would have cold-calling competitions, that I would lock myself in a room for eight hours without eating, drinking, or using the restroom and make nearly 300 phone calls and set 20 appointments. I tell the stories of how I got on airplanes to go to cities nobody else wanted to go to so I could get valuable face time with customers. I talk about all the prospecting I do in my free time to make sure I am always doing something to help the team and to make sure I make it clear to the company that they could never replace me with anyone who could be more productive than me. I say these things because they are all true stories and they are reflections on the way I am hard-wired. I don't make up any stuff, I do not ask questions in the interview for the sake of asking questions, and I do not say the things you are trained to say or the questions you are trained to ask. My philosophy is that I am only hurting myself by pretending to be someone I am not, lest I end up somewhere where the culture does not fit me and vice-versa. It is important for whoever is hiring me to like me for who I really am, and that is true for both of us. If someone thinks it is weird that I talk about the anxiety I have from growing up that informs my desire to succeed, I tell myself that it is their loss. They can hire the person instead who pretends to have some higher form of purpose and eventually learn the hard way that that person is not who they thought they were. At least when you are open and honest with people, they will know it.

There are people who I have hired who I knew I would hire within 30 seconds of meeting them simply based on their authenticity and me buying into whatever they were selling. One of the people I hired was someone who quit his first job mere months after graduating from college. He was incredibly open and honest with me about why it did not work out for him, why he was a hard worker, and why he wanted to work with me. I believed everything he had to say in large part because of the no-frills way in which he acknowledged the elephant in the room of his first gig which had gone south very quickly. If he were a con-artist, he would have made a lot of excuses for himself instead. It turned out that he is the hardest working and most adaptable person who has ever worked for me. Not a single day has ever gone by where I thought to myself that it was a bad idea to hire him because of his past experience.

This has been a fun journey. If you made it this far, I want to thank you. I hope that you took something away from this that you can apply to your sales job or your life in general. After coming all this way and preaching about the value of authenticity, I would be remiss if I did not end all of this without telling you something deeply personal.

My grandfather's death several years ago came as a bit of a shock to me. Sure, he was in his late 80s and was deteriorating pretty quickly. He had a walker and an oxygen machine. In fact, my last memory with my grandfather is me essentially being his right-hand man at a New England Patriots game back in 2014. My job was to make sure everything was functional with his oxygen machine, to help him with food and drink, and generally to assist him moving around. It was very hard for him but he was a very proud and stubborn New England sports fan who had spent many years when I was younger lamenting that he would never see the Red Sox win the World Series. So it was only fitting that the Patriots capped off one more Super Bowl win before he died in the summer of 2015.

I say it was a surprise because it was likely the result of an incident of malfeasance. I remember I was living in New York City at the time and was debating with myself if I should go see my grandfather in Massachusetts one evening or wait until the next day. An incident had just happened where he had slipped and fell because he was unsupervised and I knew he did not have much time left. I elected to wait until the following day to try and go see him one last time. That evening, I got a phone call that he had passed away. I was so mad at myself and my decision to wait a day. And though I gave him a glowing eulogy, I came to realize during his funeral that he seemed like a much more interesting person than I had ever realized, and I regretted that I had not been more intentional throughout my life trying to get to know him better. My mother and grandmother tried to calm my anxieties by telling me that I would not have wanted to see him in the state that he was in before he died, or that I could not have reasonably known what was going to happen to him, or that it was thoughtful of me to begin with to have even had the idea to try and go see him. Sometimes, no matter what someone else tells you—even if it sounds completely reasonable—it just does not seem to matter much.

This is, of course, the classic lesson of not taking anything for granted. So I thought of all the memories I had of my grandfather, large or small, in an attempt to be purposeful about them and to make sure I could keep them forever. For one thing, he was unapologetic about being who he was. He wrote letters to the editor of the local newspaper every week that gave Andy Rooney a run for his money for their curmudgeon-y takes on everything that was happening outside of the four walls of his house. If there was something to complain about, my grandfather had no issue airing his grievances for all to see, and he did not care whatsoever what people thought of him. In his pockets, he carried around a Mickey Mouse cartoon where Mickey was giving the middle finger. He needed these in case he saw someone who had done a bad job of parking their car, so he could give them his own personal brand of feedback.

But beyond being unapologetically authentic, there were also all the times growing up that he played catch with me. There was the time when he whispered in my ear one Passover where the *Afikomen* was hidden since I was the youngest child at the table. It is tradition at Passover for the children to look for a hidden piece of Matzah bread, with a prize awarded to the winner. Clearly, my grandfather wanted the underdog to win. There was the time when he and my grandmother came to my college graduation—two of very few sets of grandparents who were there that day. There is the time I interviewed him for a biography I wrote about him in high school, in which he told me that he checked the obituary every morning to make sure that he was still alive. And, of course, there is the last Patriots game.

But there is one memory of my grandfather that stands out the most. I could not have been more than ten years old, and we were sitting on a park bench in an outlet mall in The Berkshires out in Western Massachusetts. The leaves were starting to turn, I was eating an ice cream, and I had a mushroom haircut. Dozens of people were walking by around us.

"Jeffrey, you know what is amazing?" he said, tugging on my shirt to get my attention.

"What?" I asked in between licks of the ice cream.

"Look at all of these people, look at all of their faces."

I looked around.

"What about them?" I asked.

"There's billions of people all around the world, and every single one of them is different. Not a single one is the same."

Yes, all these years later, I have come to understand the beauty of that moment.

2014 at a Patriots game, the last time I saw my grandfather.

ABOUT THE AUTHOR

Jeff Kirchick is Vice President of Enterprise Sales for Next Caller, a Y-Combinator backed technology company
based out of New York City. In his role
at Next Caller, he has helped lead the
company by managing the sales team
while also selling to some of the largest companies in the world. What sets
him apart has been his ability to build
authentic relationships with his custom-

ers. He has led a successful sales career for over a decade and
spends much of his free time mentoring younger sales professionals who are interested in sales as a career, particularly those who
come from underrepresented backgrounds in tech sales.

A 2010 graduate of Princeton University, he is an avid writer
who hopes to become a screenwriter someday. In his free time, he
enjoys Boston sports (primarily the Boston Bruins), running and
exercise, collegiate wrestling, meditation, cooking, listening to
podcasts, and learning. Ultimately, what brings him joy is being
able to touch the lives of others in some meaningful way. He
currently is living in Cape Cod.

To stay in the know on Jeff's latest writing or to contact
Jeff directly, please visit JeffKirchick.com.

Made in the USA
Middletown, DE
17 December 2020

28783230R00110